The Strength In Us

The Strength In Us

Self-Help Groups In The Modern World

Written and edited by

Alfred H. Katz &
Eugene I. Bender

New Viewpoints
A Division of Franklin Watts
New York   London   1976

New Viewpoints
A Division of Franklin Watts
730 Fifth Avenue
New York, N.Y. 10019

Library of Congress Cataloging in Publication Data

Katz, Alfred Hyman, 1916–
  The strength in us.
  Includes bibliographical references and index.
  1. Self-help groups. I. Bender, Eugene I., joint author.
II. Title.
HV547.K37   361   75-23219
ISBN 0–531–05378–4
ISBN 0–531–05585–X pbk.

6 5 4 3 2 1

Contents

Acknowledgments

This book reflects the help and influence of many friends, colleagues, members of self-help organizations, and other writers. Some contributions by colleagues appear in the book as commissioned or reprinted articles, and to their authors we express our sincere thanks. But we have also had much assistance that has helped us in less tangible ways—in obtaining information about particular self-help groups, in clarifying issues relating to them, in calling relevant literature to our attention, and in reacting to early drafts or formulations.

For their indispensable help in these ways, we should like especially to thank: John Seeley, Olive Stone, Sarah Black, Joseph Eaton, Audrey Sargenia, Susan Katz, and Elizabeth Hefferin. Dr. Hefferin and Arthur Carstens supplied much of the material and formulations for Chapter 2, on self-help in history.

While we hope that all of our contributors, colleagues, friends, and readers will find value in the book, its imperfections and inadequacies are ours alone and in no way should be projected onto those who have helped us with it.

A. H. K.
E. I. B.

Part I

Self-Help
in Society—
the Motif of
Mutual Aid

There is now incontrovertible evidence that mankind has just entered upon the greatest period of change the world has ever known. The ills from which we are suffering have had their seat in the very foundations of human thought. But today something is happening to the whole structure of human consciousness. A fresh kind of life is starting.

In the face of such an upheaval, actually shaken by it, no one can remain indifferent. Swept along by the tide of affairs, what can we do to see clearly and to act decisively? No matter what reactions we may have to current events, we ought first to reaffirm a robust faith in the destiny of man.

—Pierre Teilhard de Chardin

At heart, we often wish we had the courage to drop out and recapture our real selves. The impulse to withdraw from a way of life we know to be inhuman is probably so widespread that it will become a dominant social force in the future.

To long for a human situation not subservient to the technological order is not a regressive or escapist attitude but rather one that requires a progressive outlook. . . . Since we now rarely experience anything directly and spontaneously, to achieve such a situation would require the courage to free ourselves from the constraints that prevent most of us from discovering or expressing our true nature.

—René Dubos

1

Introduction: Why Self-Help?

Underlying all the themes of this book are the difficulties of finding ways in which to live in the last third of the twentieth century in North America.

Perhaps Thoreau was wrong: most people do *not* live lives of quiet desperation. About "most" people, it seems presumptuous to generalize; but certainly *many* people in America lead lives of quiet anesthetization, and some—of desperation.

Many of the former and all the latter are seeking some anchor of stability, of connection, of faith. Throughout history people have used connections with small groups, with family and kinfolk, with peers and the like-minded, to give themselves anchorage in stormy, shifting seas; but in twentieth-century America (and elsewhere in the modern world), these connections have become critical to individual survival.

It may seem overdramatic to refer to the few hundred thousand, usually small and weak, self-help groups as *necessary* to the survival of their members. In a purely material sense, they may not be; their members would not die of hunger, exposure, or disease in the absence of these supports. But in order to continue to exist, humans need to recognize themselves and to be recognized by the society around them in all dimensions of their humanity. Survival in the modern world means more than having one's purely physical needs met; people must discover and be accepted for what they are. They need to live, to be valued, to experience, to give, to share with others, to transcend the boundaries of their own egos—to give *and* take in a social communion. Many must fight for a place in the world, to reshape a society that cannot see their value.

To us, that is why self-help groups have come into being; that is what they strive for; and that is why their importance can scarcely be measured by numbers, powers, or influence.

What conditions of social life have created and intensified the need for this type of group?

Industrialization, a money economy, the growth of vast structures of business, industry, government—all these have led to familiar specters: the depersonalization and dehumanization of institutions and social life; feelings of alienation and powerlessness; the sense, for many people, that they are unable to control the events that shape their lives; the loss of choices; feelings of being trapped by impersonal forces; the decline of the sense of community, of identity. These problems are compounded for many by the loss of belief—in the church, the state, progress, politics and political parties, many established institutions and values.

These same conditions give rise to many of the important social movements of the day—nationalism and ethnic consciousness, the civil rights struggles, Women's Liberation—all of which countertrend against the dehumanization and atomization, the discrimination and lack of nurturance in social institutions.

These dilemmas are variously expressed by novelists, playwrights, and other artists; are described in the case histories of clinicians, and, more portentously, are analyzed by social scientists.

Among the chief symptoms is an erosion of the family structure, at least in its form among Western—technologized—humanity. We are left with the "nuclear" family, which is breaking down and cannot cope successfully with burdens it formerly shared with other groupings—the tribe, the clan, the extended multigeneration instead of the one- or two-generation family.

Prominent among the explanatory truisms of the day is the "generation gap." Any middle-class parent knows it's not a gap but a grand canyon. As Theodore Roszak remarks in *The Making of a Counter-Culture*:

> *The rivalry between young and adult in Western society during the current decade is uniquely critical. . . . For better or worse, most of what is presently happening that is new, provocative, and engaging in politics, education, the arts, social relations (love, courtship, family, community) is the creation of youth who are profoundly, even fanatically, alienated from the parental generation.* [1]

From his special viewpoint, Wilhelm Reich stated this clearly:

> *The psychoanalysis of men and women of all ages, all countries, and every social class shows that: the interlacing of the socio-economic structure with the sexual structure of society and the structural reproduction of society takes place in the first four or five years and in the authoritarian family. The church only continues this function later. Thus the authoritarian state*

gains an enormous interest in the authoritarian family. It becomes the factory in which the state's ideology and structure are unfolded.[2]

A third element has emerged since Reich's classic studies of sexual repression and family structure: the effects of technology. Roszak notes Jacques Ellul's pessimistic description of technocracy:

Technique requires predictability and, no less, exactness of prediction. It is necessary then that technique shall prevail over the human being. For technique this is a matter of life and death. Technique must reduce man to a technical animal. . . . Human caprice crumbles before this necessity; there can be no human autonomy in the face of technical autonomy. The individual must be fashioned by techniques either negatively (by the techniques of understanding men) or positively (by the adaptation of man to the technical framework) in order to wipe out his personal determination into the perfect design of the organization.[3]

This analysis extends the classical motif of Adam Smith, Ricardo, and Marx in which man and his labor are viewed as a commodity, a unit in the machinery of production. Revulsion against being seen and treated as a mere commodity by the inexorable social juggernaut is the core and foundation of much contemporary dropping-out and fighting back through new social inventions.

It is fashionable among some social scientists to refer to many of the self-help groups we shall be discussing as "societies of deviants" or by a similar name, and to suggest that the "management of deviance" is their sole or chief *raison d'être*. Such analysts apparently believe that only the disenfranchised or socially stigmatized find it useful to group together in this way. Thus, in his book *Stigma*,[4] Erving Goffman refers rather contemptuously to self-help groups among the physically handicapped as "huddle-together" groups.

Such emphasis seems to us myopic; it ignores the necessity so many people find of linking themselves to others for *positive* reasons, not just defensively, but as a way of claiming an identity, of asserting themselves and finding ways to live in a society that seems stale and unnourishing to them.

Indeed, one of the common threads among the widely different groups we shall discuss is how they help people to define and grow toward an identity, toward a sense of self and purpose that is closely linked with the need for attaining a social competence.

In many cases the movement toward identity starts with a negation of existing choices. To be physically handicapped, poor, a former mental patient, or an object of exploitation or social disapproval is an identity that society forces on many unwilling "deviants." To be any of these and to feel alone is to be doubly disadvantaged.

We see self-help groups as vehicles through which these outcast persons can claim and grow toward new identities, redefining themselves and society; can overcome solitariness through identification with a reference group; and sometimes can work toward social ends or social change that they see as important.

As their efforts become viable, participants in self-help groups achieve not only subjective gains and private satisfactions: they are also helping to develop alternative structures and strategies that allow the dispossessed and the alienated to survive and to change the values of "a world they never made." Although the scale of their aspirations and operations may be limited, they are contributing to a kind of revolution, a revolution that does not conform to the classical model of a transfer of power, or the counter-cultural ideal of a transformation of personal consciousness alone, but rather one that enhances individual social competence and relationships while simultaneously affecting society's attitudes and institutions.

Many young people who reject the conventional wisdom and pieties of the family, church, and state that have molded them assert proudly their adherence to one of the streams of the counter-culture. Women previously locked into a centuries-old pattern of family walls assert the heady concepts of personal and social liberation. Blacks, browns, homosexual men and women, and prisoners and ex-convicts draw strength from one another, claim their rights to be different and to realize the promises of pluralism in the technological affluence of modern society.

In all these manifestations large gains seem to be present not only for the stigmatized, dispossessed, and "disadvantaged," but for society as a whole. New group identifications allow the forging of new identities, which in turn enlarge the sense of self and the possibilities of contributing to and altering the social order.

In the presentations that follow we hope to demonstrate and illustrate these positive aspects, among others, and to show what self-help groups *can* and do provide for their members and the society. We see them as a window on the larger social world—a human and social phenomenon that has burgeoned inevitably in answer to the malaise of our century.

Plan of the Book

In this volume, then, we direct attention to some contemporary manifestations of mutual aid and self-help as they occur in relatively small organized aggregates. In doing so, we do not deny the overwhelming everyday evidence of nonfraternalism and of fratricide and violence among individuals, families, organizations, nations, power blocs. But because the world *is* so violent, it seems useful to examine countertrends—social forces and groups that exemplify and promote cooperative and helping behavior, and which thereby enhance the chances and the capacity of the species to survive.

An undertaking of this kind might examine large collectivities —government, organized labor, industry, the military, the church, and the university—and seek to evaluate their contribution to the realization of social order through cooperation. But there is already a voluminous literature on these institutions. We have chosen to focus instead upon the much less studied, smaller, more personalized groups that offer both purpose and support to the individual and *a collective response* to an irrational and fragmented society.

Aside from passing references, we have omitted any systematic discussion of communes, although we recognize that they have undeniable salience to self-help phenomena. Space has been our major constraint in this omission; but is also clear that communes have loomed large in the public consciousness in the past few years—no fewer than a dozen books and countless articles have presented and analyzed their characteristics so fully as to render less necessary our own discussion of them.

We conceive of self-help as an integral aspect of cooperation among men. It might be more useful to discard the term *self-help* and substitute the historically sanctioned term *mutual aid,* first used by Petr Kropotkin. We suggest, however, that there are underlying differences between the primitive forms of mutual aid, which were devoted to helping members survive in a hostile or impoverished environment, and the contemporary self-help groups of post-industrial society. We view the current groups as bringing into being distinctive and new forms of egalitarian social relationships.

Surprisingly, self-help groups have been studied less often and less intently than other voluntary organizations. While self-help has been investigated as a basic human activity within the context of tribal and kinship culture, and as an element of social cohesion in formal institutions and large bureaucracies, description and *comparative analysis* of its contemporary manifestations is long overdue. The current activities, functions, aspirations, successes, and failures of self-help groups, as well as their relationships with the larger society, deserve extensive attention.

In the following pages, then, we will explore both some familiar and some uncharted terrain, concluding with what we see as the possibilities and limitations of mutual aid in contemporary society. We see ties to the past in these phenomena, historically linked to the gregarious side of man's nature. But we see as well an important future orientation in the extension of self-help into many new forms—such social innovations and movements as "free" medical clinics, consciousness-raising groups, urban and rural communes of diverse natures and styles.

Definition and Attributes of Self-Help Groups

Self-help may be an imprecise term, but it is widely used. Government agencies use it pejoratively to signify tasks that individuals or groups can undertake to promote their own well-being or community development without massive government intervention. Samuel Smiles popularized the term in a widely read tract of the Victorian age in England. Smiles, like Horatio Alger, was concerned with the workingman's solitary struggle to raise himself up by his own bootstraps through education and self-discipline. In our day, a student learning a language from records or a teaching machine is technically engaged in "self-help" but not in the sense that we use it. The general definition of self-help groups that we employ in this volume is:

> *Self-help groups are voluntary, small group structures for mutual aid and the accomplishment of a special purpose. They are usually formed by peers who have come together for mutual assistance in satisfying a common need, overcoming a common handicap or life-disrupting problem, and bringing about desired social and/or personal change. The initiators and members of such groups perceive that their needs are not, or cannot be, met by or through existing social institutions. Self-help groups emphasize face-to-face social interactions and the assumption of personal responsibility by members. They often provide material assistance, as well as emotional support; they are frequently "cause"-oriented, and promulgate an ideology or values through which members may attain an enhanced sense of personal identity.*

This definition suggests that the self-help groups we will discuss have the following attributes:

1 | Self-help always involves other persons and refers to patterned "small group" or "face-to-face" interactions.

2 | A distinguishing feature of these groups is their spontaneous origin. They arise from the active interest of the protagonists and members; organization is not imposed from without. Professionals or other authorities may have stimulated the members, initially brought them together, and given them the notion they could achieve mutual benefits. Once such groups get started the role of the sponsor, the professional, or "authority," tends to diminish or disappears altogether.

3 | Some self-help groups, either deliberately created or arising spontaneously to meet a need felt by two or more persons, are ad hoc or short-lived. Common examples are the "emergency collectivism" of neighbors in times of disasters—earthquakes,

floods, tornadoes. In these, there is a voluntary pooling of efforts to promote group survival, but they rarely continue beyond the immediate crisis. A different but currently very widespread type of transitory phenomenon is the "encounter" or "marathon" group, which has some self-help elements, but which rarely continues beyond the intensive period of interaction.

4 | Self-help groups may have a variety of functions and characteristics. The typology in Chapter 4 illustrates the varieties we have found. We make no claim that this typology is complete, but it is suggestive of the chief present forms. New social innovations or organizational forms are constantly coming into being, which may involve new functions or new combinations of existing functions. Communes of the alienated or disaffected are a current example; another are "self-help" medical clinics organized by and serving youth or women.

5 | In our view, face-to-face interaction is a key defining characteristic of self-help groups; so is *personal participation.* By these criteria, bureaucratization (for example, red tape, regimentation, and central authority) is the enemy of the self-help organization. We shall present case illustrations that point out the frequent conflicts between the original objectives of spontaneously created groups and the processes of bureaucratization—mirroring the larger society—that occur at some stage in many of them. The personal participation of members is a crucial element in preventing such a development. Mere formal membership or financial support (as in belonging to and contributing to a conservation or neighborhood improvement group) does not define the individual as a true member or participant in the kind of self-help group we are discussing.

6 | Thus, the social-psychological dimension, the meaning of participation to the individual, is one of the salient aspects of these groups. In the act of *taking part,* individuals are related, sympathetically and empathetically, to others, either peers in outlook or peers in the possession of a common problem or common need.

7 | The groups, then, supply a "reference group," a point of

connection and identification with others, a baseline for activity, a source of ego-reinforcement, a value-system by which the individual's tasks, joys, sorrows, accomplishments, and frustrations can be evaluated and dealt with. Merged or common values in the group help the previously isolated individual cope with his personal situations *vis-à-vis* the social colossus.

8| Basic to our concept of the self-help group is the assumption that its members agree upon and engage in some *actions*. Such behavior may be directed at the community, at social institutions, at personal change (as in "encounter" or transactional therapy groups), at learning something—a body of knowledge or a skill. There is always an acknowledged *purpose* in coming together; the aims of this kind of group are more than merely social interaction. An agenda emerges, whether narrow or broad. Often the group's program is utilitarian and specific, such as encompassing a means by which the individual is helped to cope with and overcome a *handicap*, stigma, or other personal difficulty perceived by the member himself, by the group, and/or by the larger society.

9| Typically, self-help groups start from a condition of powerlessness; no matter what they may later achieve, their initial resources are always limited, and the exercise and control of power is not one of their immediate objects. This differentiates them in our eyes from "mutual aid" groupings and agreements among those who exercise political or economic or juridical power—cartels and corporation boards, "old boy" networks and friendship cliques that sustain political domination and privilege or withhold it from the disenfranchised and divided plebeians.

It can be seen from these defining attributes that in our usage self-help groups are to be distinguished from voluntary membership "service organizations" oriented to traditional philanthropy, such as the Shriners. They differ, too, from organized political parties that operate on a precinct level and from political interest groups, such as the League of Women Voters, that carry on educational activities. Nor are they merely activity groups set up to learn or share a skill, craft, or hobby. Rather, peer-related support groups may share *some* of the interests of such voluntary organizations but retain distinctiveness by combining emotional sustenance with a variety of program activities.

In the pages that follow we will discuss the characteristics of the self-help phenomena as they are now observable in North America and in other countries. We shall attempt to place the groups in historical context. We will seek to account for their successes and failures and to analyze the external and internal factors that affect them. We shall assess the groups in their relationships to the wider society and will speculate about their role in "welfare state" and in "post-industrial" societies.

The meagerness of empirical research on the subject of self-help groups has long puzzled the writers, but we have scanned whatever literature exists. In this book, we reprint case and analytical materials that illustrate our themes, some descriptive and statistical data from pertinent studies and accounts, and we seek to indicate where additional information is needed before conclusions can be drawn.

We recognize that we are mounting a large canvas, but our goal is modest: to paint with broad brush strokes, limning in the contours of a major phenomenon. In the interests of scope and topicality we realize that we have at times sacrificed some detail and depth. While this work is essentially aimed at synthesizing present knowledge, we have sought to provide a framework in the light of which deeper analyses and hypotheses can be generated and tested. If we stimulate both social scientists and the interested public to a greater awareness of self-help phenomena, we shall have achieved our aims.

In the life of a group just as in the life of an individual, the capacity for self-help and the need for help from others are determined by the *whole situation* in which the group is living: the strength of its individual members, the strength and character of the relations between the group members, the reality problems which confront the group, the relations of the group with the neighboring groups and the state, etc. All these factors together determine how much, in a given situation, the group will be able to do itself and whether and how much help from the outside world will be needed.[1]

—J. F. De Jongh

2

Self-Help and Mutual Aid in History

Introduction

A definitive history of mutual aid and self-help—embracing social ideas, organizational forms, people and movements—has not yet been written. Early in this century, Petr

Kropotkin[2] sketched the outlines of mutual aid in Europe from primitive times to the beginning of the twentieth century. Although original and powerful, his work has had few followers.

This chapter briefly summarizes Kropotkin's analysis and extends the record to contemporary North America by calling attention to some developments in mutual aid since the colonial period.

Linking the present to the past, we may generalize that the major impetus for mutual aid and self-help has come from the poor, the underprivileged, the powerless. In our day, when material deprivations or physical dangers are not as acute as in the past, we find that self-help movements are also generated by the human need for emotional sustenance, through day-to-day interaction with the like-minded.

Although the forms and applications of self-help ideas vary widely, a quick tour through history helps us to understand that self-help forms are no new thing but have provided over the ages a common source for individual identity and support.

To review the role of mutual aid in human history requires that we note a basic paradox of man's existence. Like all living creatures, *Homo sapiens* initially seeks to satisfy his biological needs and to ensure his personal survival. But biological survival depends largely upon the cooperation and assistance of other humans, and man, who is also a social being, is committed to living in a society through which he and his fellows attain individual and common goods.

History, from one viewpoint, is the record of compromises between individual and social commitments, so that men simultaneously meet their own needs and contribute to the maintenance of the needs of society. Despite a plethora of violence, wars, indignities, and inhumanity, there is also a long history of human benevolence and cooperative action, which shows that man's striving to live harmoniously with his fellows has been as persistent as the Hobbesian struggle for personal dominance and advantage.

Early Mutual Aid

In very primitive societies, the struggle to survive in a hostile environment eliminated most weaker or less fit members. Nevertheless, historians of prehistory—anthropologists and archaeologists—have shown that even preliterate societies had conceptions of justice and cooperative action. Tribes or clan members grouped together in mutual aid, to "cast out" or protect the less fit, to defend against or to attack other tribes.

Petr Kropotkin, the great authority on this aspect of early history, traced the consequences of mutual aid in Darwinian terms: animal species that survived were both the fittest and had rudimentary mutual aid practices. Man's survival depended on his development of the habits of social cooperation—in food gathering and sharing, child rearing, land use, and the maintenance of defense against marauders. These primitive forms of mutual assistance became threatened, according to Kropotkin, at the time of the creation of families.

Small clans preserved themselves only as long as there were no separate families; with family-kinship systems came individual accumulation and the hereditary transmission of wealth and power. The loosening of tribal bonds was inevitable. Weaker clans split off and disintegrated; the stronger clans formed a social organization of a new type—the village community—where membership bonds were based on communal ownership and mutual protection of the village territory.

These early village communities were the precursors of the medieval compounds and cities, which had respective complexes of laws, cultures, territorial boundaries, and social hierarchies. Through the Dark Ages, when city-state autocracies arose, the state power sought to eradicate the fraternal or communal activity based on the earlier mutual aid principles. But Kropotkin believes that the efforts to suppress mutual aid did not succeed; it remained at least a covert motif of social life.

By the Middle Ages, cooperative action and mutual aid were again distinguishable. In cooperative action a community could organize its members to build a defensive barrier against invaders, to take up collections of food, or to supply shelter or other assistance for needy members. In the classical form of mutual aid, neighbors might join together to save the harvest of an ailing fellow farmer. The mutual aid pattern could also be found in the activities of various groups in the community: trade guilds, culture groups, social orders, whose members shared a common problem, occupation, or custom and who sought common protection against outsiders.

The history of the Freemasons is instructive in this regard. Previously a craft guild of stonemasons, it reorganized after the Black Death had devastated European social life in the fourteenth century to provide a supportive social anchor for its members against the privations and confusions of the times. Informal groupings—secret societies and mutual aid groups—provided constant resistance and refuge for members against the repressions of a theocratic or autocratic state.

The Beginnings of Mutual Aid in Modern Europe

Up to this point in human history mutual aid involved not only cooperative efforts to solve a problem, but also was largely exclusive—the aid would be extended only to bona fide members of the in-group. Strangers, travelers, the physically or mentally disabled, and others needy of refuge or succor and lacking the support of a group had to rely on the meager charity the town might occasionally and temporarily provide. Most of the refuges that existed in this era—the so-called xenodochia—were established and maintained under church auspices and were independent of the communities themselves.

By the beginning of the sixteenth century a number of political and social factors were emerging that were soon to change the character of European social life. Notable among these were the Protestant challenge to Catholic dominance in government and the increasing mobility of the population, which partly stemmed from enclosure acts and the burgeoning of domestic industry under primitive capitalism. There was also concern over the inadequacies of the local and state machinery and of the church charities in dealing with the uncomfortable and rebellious poor. In England, where these social and political conflicts were first noted, Elizabethan Poor Laws were passed between 1601 and 1605, requiring each parish to provide for and to contain its own poor. The Poor Laws equated disability and poverty with crime and controlled less fortunate individuals through disenfranchisement, public punishment, and incarceration.

In the following centuries, the Poor Laws were amended many times, ultimately extending statutory welfare and health benefits to all citizens on evidence of need. However, stringent means tests, workhouses, and almost-starvation-level relief funds minimized the effectiveness of such practices. Long before this point was reached in the twentieth century, industrialization and the prevailing laissez-faire philosophy produced an exponentially expanding chaos of social, economic, and health problems in an ever-growing population.[3] Remedial attempts included the establishment of philanthropic and government programs for the needy; the onus, however, remained with the pauper to prove his inability to obtain employment. Thus the way was hastened for the spontaneous development of schemes of mutual aid by groups of industrial workers.

In the nineteenth century in England, Friendly Societies were a significant return to mutual aid principles in the lower classes' efforts to cope with adverse living conditions. Originating spontaneously as local groups of workers sought collective support against the exigencies of financial need, illness, or death, the Friendly Societies set up special funds for members through crisis periods. Members could also borrow for the repair or building of a home, to purchase a cow, or to stock a small business. Most of the Friendly Societies' concrete benefits were thus provided through an early cooperative form of insurance.

Lord Beveridge describes the societies as "organizations for brotherly aid in misfortune and channels for the spirit of voluntary services, as well as being agencies for mutual insurance and personal saving."[4] That this movement for mutual aid was meeting a popular need was evidenced by the fact that by the turn of the twentieth century some 27,000 Friendly Societies existed in Britain. They covered nearly every aspect of English social life, including the varied forms of housing and building societies, farm trading and cooperatives, workmen's compensation, cattle insurance, loans, thrifts, investments, fine arts, cooperative stores, fraternal and social collectives, and many others. Although the later nationalization of health and minimum income systems in England reduced the role and importance of the Friendly Societies, many have continued to exist, not only because of members' needs for financial assistance above the state-determined mini-mums, but also to retain old community and friendship ties.

Producer-Consumer Cooperatives

Another nineteenth-century self-help innovation, consumer co-operation, is also a product of the Industrial Revolution. Unlike the Friendly Societies, consumer cooperatives are not exclusive-ly an English phenomenon, although they developed earlier there because the Industrial Revolution showed earlier definition in the British Isles. Evidence of early types of cooperatives has been found in other European countries.[5] Swiss dairymen, for exam-ple, have made cheese cooperatively since the Middle Ages. Joint stock companies in Spain, Portugal, France, and Holland origin-ated as means to support the costs of voyages of exploration and colonization.

Nevertheless, the English experience in producer and con-sumer cooperatives, for example, the Rochdale Society, is partic-ularly noteworthy. Weavers, shoemakers, and other craftsmen cooperatively purchased supplies and consumer goods; their ex-ample had far-reaching influence in Europe and later in North America.

Mutual Aid in the United States

The early American colonists initially followed the pattern of mutual aid through the spontaneous neighborliness of small com-munities. They banded together both to produce necessities and for protection against nature and hostile Indians. But this phase was short-lived: the fertility of the land and the freedom from oppressive state controls led to the abandonment of communal effort in agriculture and crafts and its replacement by the marked individualism of production and ownership that has characterized American society ever since.

Mutual aid principles, however, were not entirely lost: colo-nists assisted one another in such farming chores as crop seeding and harvesting, home and barn raising, and other shared tasks. Throughout the eighteenth and nineteenth centuries the frontiers could not have been explored and conquered and the wilderness tamed without the defense of homestead and land claims through common efforts against both the environment and the constant encroachments of railroad and other monopolies.

As the problems of town and rural living grew more complex, self-help forms emerged to meet common difficulties. By 1800, groups of dairymen had formed mutual assistance associations to purchase fodder for stock and to ensure markets for their products. Irrigation cooperatives developed in a number of areas, such as those of the Mormons who pooled labor and capital to bring water to the dusty Utah lands.[6]

By the mid-1800's, most of the clamant ills of the Industrial Revolution were manifest in the United States: long working hours, low wages, child labor, illness, unemployment, overcrowded and unsanitary cities, and the like. Revulsion and revolt took a number of forms. One was to create utopian cooperative villages or communes; the best known of these were the Fanny Wright and Owenite societies that sprang up in the 1820's. Their proposed remedy was the formation of cooperatives having land and tools sufficient for the support of members.

Trade Unions and Mutual Aid

The campaigns for better living conditions also led to the formation of trade unions. When simple organization for collective bargaining failed to improve their members' lives, some unions organized nonprofit stores through which members could buy necessities more cheaply than on the open market. But these early union attempts at mutual aid did not survive the counterpressures of poor leadership, repressive legislation, and the disruptions of the Civil War.

A stronger wave of cooperative activity arose in response to the postwar depression of the late 1860's. Soldiers returning to impoverished farms and urban unemployment sought new opportunities in the still-virginal West. Joined by unprecedented numbers of city unemployed and European immigrants, their efforts produced in the 1870's an all-time high in agricultural output. But a bitter price was paid—calamitous drops in market prices and high transportation costs ruined many farmers and led to the loss of their lands.[7]

In the 1870's a league of consumer cooperatives, the Sovereigns of Industry, emerged. This movement was taken over by the Knights of Labor, the first industrial union, which, in turn, added producers cooperatives. The cooperative movement flourished for some years; at its peak unions were supporting some 135 cooperative societies.

Most of these cooperatives failed for reasons of economics, legal difficulties in obtaining state charters, and public hostility to groups associated with the labor movement.

Unionists and their leaders continued to hunger after means of ensuring economic security. Programs of mutual benefit to members could be supported by dues and per capita taxes. Thus the Molders, Spinners and Typographical Workers set up union-financed health and pension plans as early as the 1860's. The unwillingness of commercial companies to insure the Railroad Engineers forced that union to develop its own insurance plan. Later, it pioneered in a home for disabled and retired engineers, and in 1912 it developed one of the country's first union-sponsored pension programs. Many other unions followed suit.[8]

For a time another experiment in concrete self-help engaged the interests of many unions. Practical-minded unionists argued that workers should join hands and emulate the capitalists, who were successful and powerful. Organizing a bank was seen as a step toward this goal. Despite Samuel Gompers' efforts to dissuade them, the so-called practical unionists persisted, and from 1904 through 1924 a proposal supporting the organization of Union Labor Banks was regularly introduced at each labor convention.

In 1920 the International Association of Machinists purchased the majority stock of a Washington bank. Later the Locomotive Engineers founded a bank, and within a few years unions owned thirty-six banks with resources of more than $136 million.

In the late twenties and early thirties, unions also began to focus on housing for members. The Amalgamated Clothing Workers took the lead in organizing cooperative housing projects. Some union-sponsored housing programs proved outstandingly successful in meeting members' needs on a cooperative basis.

Workers' Education

Another area of unionist self-help is the twentieth-century movement for workers' education. Born in the social ferment of the early 1900's, and reflecting uneasiness over the rapid growth of corporate power and the dehumanization of the conditions of employment, adult education was seen as a way to improve both the workplace and the workers' neighborhoods.

In Great Britain the Workers' Education Association was organized in 1903, and in the United States the Women's Trade Union League established a school for women workers in New York in 1905.[9]

The movement spread to the Midwest and the frontier, where workers, farmers, and cattlemen joined together in classes to discuss economic and social issues. Oscar Ameringer, a well-known Wisconsin journalist, reports visiting an encampment in Oklahoma where hundreds of settlers from scattered homesteads took part in a week-long discussion of economics and politics. A textbook, *The Struggle for Existence,* served as a basis for the discussion, which emphasized radical alternatives to the corporate system. The hope was that through education some means could be found to build a more human and cooperative society.

In 1916 the International Ladies' Garment Workers' Union established an education department; the Amalgamated Clothing Workers soon followed suit. Both these union programs emphasized the need for major social reforms.

The Great Depression of the 1930's stimulated the formation of a variety of workers' education institutions on a regional basis. Among these experiments were the Brookwood Labor College, Commonwealth College, and the Highlander Folk School in the Southeast.

An experiment in "people education" on a self-help model, the Highlander School's original purpose was "to change society fundamentally by educating for a revolution which could basically alter economic and political power relations to the advantage of poor and powerless people." While the purpose was utopian, a style of mutual learning characterized Highlander from the outset. A basic axiom is an application of self-help ideas: learn from the South's depressed people and help black and white to help themselves.[10]

Highlander, which is still in existence today, operates on the premise that individualism alienates and divides, emphasizing, instead, the social instincts that lead to cooperation and collective solutions. The Highlander "method" utilizes residential workshops in a home-primary group setting. Education is always aimed at collective action programs to benefit a neighborhood, a community, a city, the southern region. Participants in Highlander workshops are encouraged to carry out a continuous process of education in their home communities so that true peer learning and group problem-solving can result.

Summary

Historically, the essence of mutual aid has been the need for and creation of group coping mechanisms that ensure man's survival in the face of environmental threats and deprivations. There have been many patterns of group action. Sometimes the coming together for mutual aid resulted in highly structured organizations like the Masons, Friendly Societies, or cooperatives. In other cases mutual aid remained casual and informal, the self-help groups retaining vitality through their very smallness and looseness of structure.

In earliest history the family and a small group of neighbors constituted the primary resources for mutual aid. Even as populations grew larger and societies more complex, families and kinship groups not only preferred but also were expected to care for their ill, aged, and disabled; to be dependent upon public charity was sinful and pitiable.

With the onset of the Industrial Revolution, neither the Poor Laws nor later governmental reforms could prevent or adequately solve many of the problems of increasing population size and density: poverty, delinquency, social maladjustment, ill health. Only a minority of people had access to the newer but still sparse forms of mutual assistance in an industrial society, such as cooperatives and communes. Most of the socially needy had to seek aid from whatever sources were available: neighbors, private or parochial charities, and public relief. But as our quick review has shown, men with like needs and goals persistently seek each other out, no matter what the historical circumstances. The problems of the time and the focus of mutual aid differ widely, but the constant element is men's need to give and take help from one another.

In our own day, these needs seem to have reached a crescendo.

The few decades since the end of World War II have witnessed an unprecedented flowering in North America of the greatest number and variety of self-help groups ever known in human history. Many of the social ills and alienating forces that produced Friendly Societies in the Great Britain of the 1870's are not only reproduced but also magnified many times in the North America of the 1970's. And the contemporary self-help groups reveal much more strongly than in the past a distinct polarity in response to the pervasive individualist ethos: both social change and individual or self-change are now prevalent motifs of equal strength and significance.

Moreover, there is another element that seems to inform present self-help activities: a spirit of hope that man can master his own life and not merely remain the captive of intractable forces.

This optimistic spirit appears part of the worldwide trend toward self-determination and nationalism, predicated upon faith in the ability of common people to set up a satisfying social order through their own efforts.

To the extent that a voluntary association has a "mission," it can be referred to as a social movement.

—Hans Toch

3

Self-Help as a Social Movement

"When people feel themselves abandoned or frustrated by conventional society, they can sometimes bypass established institutions and create informal organizations 'on the side.' Such grass-roots movements serve to provide otherwise unavailable services, to protest indignities, to escape suffering, to relieve tension, to explain confusing events, or in some way to create a more tolerable way of life than is afforded by existing formal organizations.''

These reflections by Hans Toch, author of *The Social Psychology of Social Movements,*[1] can serve as an introduction to the motivations of those seeking membership and a meaningful experience in groups as diverse as Parents without Partners, Synanon, Gamblers Anonymous, Recovery, Inc., the Fortune Society, Alcoholics Anonymous (A.A.), Widow-to-Widow, and many others.

Taken alone, membership figures convey neither the social significance of self-help groups nor their relationship to contemporary social movements. Nevertheless, the sheer quantitative aspects of these groups are worth highlighting. The National Association for Retarded Children counted 1,300 local units by the end of 1968, embracing a membership of more than 130,000. The United Cerebral Palsy Association of America has some 260 local units, a membership exceeding 100,000, and more than 50,000 year-round active volunteers, plus several hundred thousand additional volunteers during fund-raising drives. The Muscular Dystrophy Association of America claims more than 400 chapters and 500,000-plus volunteers. Other self-help groups in the "disease specific" field include the National Cystic Fibrosis Foundation with 152 local affiliates and the National Hemophilia Foundation with 52 state units.[2] Alcoholics Anonymous, together with its auxiliary groups, has membership exceeding 350,000, excluding nonreported members, in some 12,500 chapters throughout the world.[3]

In 1963, Maurice Jackson compiled a directory of 265 groups formed by persons with a common problem and usually performing multiple services for their members on a local level, outside the framework of the usual community services.[4] A more recent example are the Welfare Rights organizations in the United States and Canada, embracing at least 40,000 participants in local affiliates throughout most states and provinces.[5]

The explosive growth of these groups requires explanation, since they clearly constitute a social event of magnitude. The self-help movement might have received greater attention from the media during the 1960's were it not for the crisis and agonies of the Vietnam War and the civil rights struggles. Yet three decades ago, self-help groups in their contemporary forms, with the singular exception of A.A., were virtually unknown. After immigration to North America had slowed to a trickle, and in the period of the Great Depression, many of the previously important self-help and mutual aid fraternal organizations—burial and loan societies, ethnic insurance associations, *landsmanshaften*—declined or disappeared altogether, having been organized chiefly to serve the needs of immigrants and their second-generation offspring. But, as our chapter on history shows, immediately after World War II there was a significant flowering of newer types of self-help groups. Some reasons for their emergence will be examined in the light of social movement theory.

Social Movements and Change

"The essence of a social movement is change," wrote William B. Cameron, adding that "the main characteristic of a social movement is that it seeks to change the culture or change the social structure or redistribute the power of control within a society."[6]

Many people, working alone or in concert with others, desire change—on a personal or a social level, or both. On a personal level, some succeed by changing a spouse, a job, residence, or more broadly, a life-style. On a social level, they may campaign in elections or for educational reform. But not all changes, even in the extrapersonal sphere, involve a relationship with a social movement. The converse, however, seems demonstrably true: all social movements, successful or not, lead to some changes in the social order, alterations in the personality and consciousness of the participant, or both.

A classic definition of social movements views them as "collective enterprises to establish a new order of life."[7] Do *all* self-help groups then seek a new order, and may they all qualify as social movements under that definition? To answer these questions involves discussion of the "how," "what," and "why" of social movements in general, and of their "interfacing" with self-help groups in particular.

Ralph Turner[8] has provocatively singled out three major themes of the representative social movements that have flourished since the French Revolution and that still characterize the contemporary scene. These themes are (1) political-humanitarianism, (2) material-economic, and (3) psychological-therapeutic.

The first theme was clearly embodied in the French, American, and subsequent European revolutions that overthrew the aristocracies of these countries, while attempting to lay the foundations for the political forms of representative democracy. The second of these themes was most clearly articulated in the United States and Canada by the struggles of labor and immigrant groups in forming unions, cooperatives, and other vehicles to secure social justice through the redistribution of national resources, income, goods, and services. The third theme involves demands for psychological meaning in life, for personal dignity and identity, and for self-actualization.

We find the psychological-therapeutic theme particularly embodied in many current groups such as homosexuals and ex-prisoners, today viewed by society and themselves as less "deviant" than formerly. Our observations suggest that this motif is a more pervasive component of social movements today than at any time in the past. As a corollary, their members insist on a more "open" style of relationships, more informal communication, less formal organizational and authority structures than have existed in social movements of earlier times.

These desires seem linked to a "change" orientation. When compared with black power, ecology, student power, and other broad "causes," the assertiveness of self-help movements appears relatively muted. But as our historical discussion demonstrates, *self-help as a social movement* has been continuously change-oriented.

The historical evidence indicates that the basis for self-help, like other social movements, is found in discontent with present living conditions. As we have seen, the individual's search for personal satisfaction and identity, which leads him to affiliate with self-help groups, takes place today under fiercely difficult and alienating conditions. Changing technologies and the increasing inadequacy of formal institutions motivate a search for more satisfying life-styles. Thus, contemporary self-help organizations and social movements involve different formats, challenges, and rewards than were found in the past.

The nature of the rewards to members of self-help groups will be elaborated in later chapters on structure and dynamics. There is a wide diversity of beliefs among self-help group members as to what changes will be meaningful for them. But, in general, it is clear that *self-help as a social movement is by its very nature change-directed,* seeking alterations (1) in its constituency's relationship to society per se, (2) in dominant institutions of the society, and, often, (3) in the personality and behavior of the member himself.

Types of Social Movements

Herbert Blumer analyzes social movements under three headings: general, specific, and expressive.

General social movements, such as those for mental health, peace, or Women's Liberation, seek to bring about changes in people's values, both of their members and the public at large. Such movements are often marked by an *absence* of (1) established leadership, (2) a recognized membership, and (3) clear structural forms for guidance and control. Informality, inconspicuousness, and subterraneanity prevail.

Specific social movements—Black Muslims, Townsend Movement, the Industrial Workers of the World (I.W.W.)—are identified by well-defined objectives, which their adherents see as not only desirable but also *achievable.* Such groups become microcosms of the larger society, embodying a recognized leadership, a "we-consciousness" atmosphere, meaningful traditions and values. They are marked by a division of labor and develop a social structure and a status hierarchy. A diminution of impulsive and informal behavior leads to eventual formalization and institutionalization.

The degree to which such specific social movements resist or support changes in the social order and the restructuring of established social institutions is one important way of classifying them. A similarity in the classification of self-help groups and special social movements appears in the writings of Alfred Katz and Edward Sagarin. Katz classifies self-help groups according to whether their goals and the means by which these are achieved *uphold* (Assimilative Groups) or *contravene* (Assertive Groups) the normative order of society.[9] Sagarin analyzes the ways in which a variety of self-help groups are perceived by *external* populations, as well as in what manner *internally* the members view themselves as deviant from established institutions and dominant cultural patterns.[10]

Expressive social movements, Herbert Blumer's third category, manifest the following traits: (1) intense intimacy and esprit de corps, (2) exaltation and ecstasy accompanied by prophetic utterances, (3) projection of collective feelings on, and bestowal of a sacred meaning to, outside objects—persons, behaviors, songs, artifacts, (4) the development in sect and cultlike terms of a creed, a ritual, a viable theology, and (5) the fortification of the movement through proselytizing for converts.

Several of these traits, in varying intensity, appear to typify such organizations as A.A. and its imitators, Synanon and the X-Kalay Foundation (1, 3, 4, 5). The founder of Recovery, Inc., Abraham Low, initiated a rigid methodology for the mentally troubled, including former mental patients, to cope with their day-to-day problems, which appears to embody traits 1, 3, and 4.

A number of self-help groups, founded on principles of mutual aid, in both earlier and later periods of their growth, seem to incorporate these attributes of specific and expressive social movements. The *minimal* conditions social scientists have found essential for social movements to arise appear in self-help groups superficially as different as Operation Bootstrap, Seventh Step, Parents without Partners, and parent-child preschool cooperatives. These conditions include the following:

There must be some source of dissatisfaction arising from a person's day-to-day living pattern.

These discontents are shared with others and not merely internalized as private agendas to be reckoned with at some future, unspecified date.

The dissatisfaction contains an element of deprivation, *otherwise collective action is unlikely to occur.*

The individual perceives that some possessed quality *(status, power, material goods, social acceptance) has been taken away or withheld when it is his due.* [11]

The Self-Help Component in Social Movements

It is not unusual for social movements to concern themselves with self-help activities in order to satisfy their members' needs. Thus, Women's Liberation chapters in U.S. and Canadian cities are currently sponsoring abortion information centers, consciousness-raising groups, and self-help medical services. Various civil rights movements arrange bail and maintenance for activists arrested in demonstrations. Special social movements like the Black Muslims consciously foster mutual aid sentiments and activities among their members. *But social movements in which self-help activities constitute a core of the movement's activities are an exception rather than a rule.* The explanation for this apparent paradox is not hard to find. A major force motivating members to join self-help groups lies in their expectation of immediate and concrete benefits for themselves. In contrast, persons identifying with other social movements are in general prepared to *defer gratifications* until the movement has brought about *societal changes,* which in turn may bring altered or enhanced personal satisfactions. There is, however, some evidence to suggest that the counter-culture, whose ideology extols and embodies self-help principles, provides a significant departure from this behavioral style, particularly for youth groups. Immediate gratification of the senses becomes a goal rather than a means for the attainment of personal and group salvation. A number of self-help groups respond to this counter-culture "ideological force-field"; in this sense they are part of the larger, vaguely parametered human potential movement.

Hans Toch writes that one variant form of a social movement is that distinguished by its "gain through community." He describes self-help groups such as Take Off Pounds (TOPS), Recovery, Inc., and Alcoholics Anonymous as fitting this model. His analysis serves as a point of departure for the posing of an important question: What links exist between well-known specific social movements, such as the Black Panther Party or pro-abortion groups, and the many addiction or disease-centered groups that have made their way into public consciousness? This question can be answered by a series of propositions distilled from our observations, which clarify the connections, similarities, and differences between the two kinds of phenomena:

1|To the extent that a social movement seeks "self-help" as *personal* change for its members it can be viewed as a self-help group.

Thus, Edward Sagarin[10] describes the tendency of stigmatized persons with physical abnormalities and emotional handicaps to form self-help groups for two major purposes: (1) as a means of enabling members to conform more easily to societal norms or (2) to create new standards that will accommodate their nonconformist behavior. The first purpose may be seen as an example of self-change. The second, the group's struggle for *rights* as against privileges, their rejection of the concept of stigma, and their mutual reinforcement of deviant values, points to a greater acceptance of the worthwhile aspects of self, in turn implying self-change in attitudinal and possibly behavioral terms.

2|The extent to which a social movement stresses socialization and interpersonal interaction among its members, to the minimization of the movement's overall goals, aids in its classification as a self-help group.

3|To the extent that a social movement permits and enhances ongoing face-to-face relationships on an egalitarian basis, with continuous participation in decision making, the social movement approximates a self-help organization.

While some self-help associations encompass large memberships, a formal bureaucratic apparatus, status concerns, and so forth, the influencing of public opinion and the search for converts are *secondary* to the mutual aid extended from one person to another. *Their volunteers essentially serve their own community of participants.*

4|To the extent that "white-collar" salaried administrators, degree-holding "social therapists," or other professionals are *not* instrumental in the social movement, the movement resembles a self-help group.

5|The degree to which people are brought to social movements because of their preexisting problems rather than through the skill of agitators and leaders, as well as the extent to which the problems are seen as ends in themselves instead of as means to the broader goals of the movement, brings the movement into greater accord with the self-help form.

6|To the extent that a social movement "graduates" members from its midst when satisfactory social skills have been acquired and the extent to which the movement supplies a ceremonial "rites of passage" to the larger society, does the social movement most nearly approximate a self-help organization.

Groups such as Parents without Partners (upon remarriage of the single member), the X-Kalay Foundation, and the Fortune Society (see Part II) regard it as desirable that their adherents "graduate" to the wider community, both for their own sake and to convince others that the self-help group can provide assistance or even salvation.

7|The extent to which a self-help group, organized around a specific social or individual disability, cooperates with other self-help groups organized to combat different disabilities reinforces the social movement aspect of the self-help group.

An example of such cooperation between separate self-help groups is found commonly in affiliates of Overeaters Anonymous, where A.A. literature is distributed regularly at meetings, the two groups frequently exchange guest speakers, and a considerable number of members belong to both groups simultaneously.

The Aspirations of Potential Members

When a potential recruit to a *personal growth* type of self-help social movement commits himself to joining, he acts on two assumptions: (1) the group will help solve his problems more effectively than he can himself and (2) the goals of a particular group—its ideology and socialization, its programs and procedures—are compatible with his view of his own needs and outlook. This type of group also can reinforce the new member's belief that personal "action" is important, that the action possibilities are feasible and attainable, and that there is an incentive-reward system and norms by which he can measure his progress. Toch speaks to this issue: "Each individual's efforts to solve his own problems becomes part of his efforts to solve a social problem."[12]

The confluence between self-help groups and social movements is found both from the group's and the individual's point of view in this dynamic interplay between personal and social change. Social movements that ascribe individual difficulties to the play of social forces are nevertheless called upon to render concrete benefits to their members. Conversely, self-help groups that stress self-actualization, when viewed in a broad perspective, take on in aggregate the character of a social movement. Any major differences between the genesis and maintenance of these social forces may well hinge upon the following: Individuals who desire self-change tend to be *less animated* by the politics of protest and instead withdraw into religio-cultist settings as the *crucial* means of changing society or themselves. In citizenship terms, as discussed elsewhere, they are *emotional activists rather than political activists.*[13]

Self-change movements are now beginning to evoke the intense scrutiny and research that was formerly reserved for better-known social movements. In the coming years sizable research efforts will be expended upon self-change, noninstitutionalized, and nonestablishment entities. This type of self-help group seems to be discarding the ideological elements found in the more publicized contemporary movements and replacing them with a diffuse but effective quasi-ideological aim—that of self-renewal and self-actualization through mutual aid.

Part II

Self-Help
Organizations:
Themes and
Variations

4

Toward a Classification of Self-Help Groups

There may be as many as half a million self-help groups in the United States. The numbers, importance, and scope of the groups has grown so markedly in recent years that any attempt to catalog them would be futile. Hardly a week passes without word of the creation of a new self-help group by persons having in common an obscure and previously neglected problem. It was not thought surprising when parents of the thalidomide victims of a decade ago organized themselves into a special group concerned with both securing medical care and education for their children and obtaining financial redress from the drug manufacturers whose product had created the problem.

But it may be surprising to learn that in Los Angeles County a group called Parents Anonymous was formed. Made up of mothers who had committed physical assaults upon their children ("battered babies"), its members sought help from one another in understanding and changing themselves;[1] their efforts have stimulated the growth of a national organization.

Given their numbers and extraordinary diversity, their spontaneous creation and frequent early demise, it is a difficult task to tease out and to analyze the common threads in those organizations that we believe embody self-help characteristics. These groups may range from a drug-approving and drug-oriented commune to an antidrug social movement such as Synanon, and still, in our view, exemplify the self-help form and utilize self-help principles.

Classification, however, is necessary to analyze and understand their differences and similarities. In this chapter we attempt several ways of classifying the confusing universe of self-help groups.

The typology that we have found most useful and that will be employed throughout this book breaks down the groups according to what we perceive as their primary focus:

1|*Groups that are primarily focused on self-fulfillment or personal growth.* These are often referred to by themselves and others as "therapeutic" (as in the American Federation of Therapeutic Self-Help Clubs). A good example of this type of self-help group is Recovery, Inc., which is dealt with in the study by Donald T. Lee in Chapter 5.

2|*Groups that are primarily focused on social advocacy.* We use this term rather than the more usual "social action," because it is broader. Advocacy includes agitating and education directed at existing institutions, professionals, the public; confrontation, muckraking, and social crusading. It can be both on behalf of broad issues, such as legislation, the creation of new services, change in the policies of existing institutions and so on, or it can be on behalf of individuals, families, or other small groups. Typically, such groups as Welfare Rights organizations and the Committee for the Rights of the Disabled use both kinds of advocacy.

3|*Groups whose primary focus is to create alternative patterns for living.* Group solidarity provides a foundation for society's changing social institutions and attitudes. These groups may start new living and working alternatives of their own. Individual growth and self-fulfillment is obtained in the process but is not the primary group goal. Examples are Women's Liberation, Gay Liberation, and Operation Bootstrap.

4|*"Outcast haven"* or *"rock·bottom"* groups. These groups provide a refuge for the desperate, who are attempting to secure personal protection from the pressures of life and society, and thereby to save themselves from mental or physical decline. This type of group involves total commitment in a living-in arrangement (a sheltered environment), with a close, if not twenty-four-hour-a-day, supervision by peers or persons who have successfully grappled with similar problems of their own. An example of this type of group is the X-Kalay Foundation in Vancouver, British Columbia (discussed in Chapter 7), and in its beginnings but, in our view, not at present, the Synanon Foundation.

Some Other Classifications

In addition to the typology presented above, other ways of classifying the groups have been attempted. Thus, Edward Sagarin, writing in the current vein of the sociology of deviance, makes a distinction between two types of groups that adopt different solutions to the management of deviance. In the first, typified by A.A., "the deviant may escape from stigma by conforming to the norms of the society; that is, by 'reforming,' by relinquishing the stigmatizing behavior.''

In the second type of group, exemplified by homophile organizations such as the Gay Liberation Front, the deviant "may escape from stigma by reforming the norms of society, by reducing the sanctions against his behavior; that is, by changing, not himself, but the rule-making others."[2]

Another dimension of classification is to distinguish between groups that are predominantly inward-turning and member-centered, devoted to the interests, narrowly conceived, of their own immediate participants, and those groups that have a main focus of interest outside their participants or members and are directed at social or mass goals, that is, the reform of the welfare system, democratization of the army, and so forth.

An *inner-focused* group may be particularly helpful to its members in material benefits, provide opportunities for personal growth, give emotional and social support, and offer many specific, concrete services.

Outer-focused groups, whose predominant interest is outside the immediate welfare of their members, mainly devoted to changing legislation or social policy, often have less meaning to their members than do inner-focused groups, and their member participation is usually less intense and consistent.

Still another characteristic by which self-help groups can be usefully compared has to do with their degree of acceptance of the prevailing, dominant cultural and social values. For example, most of the "anonymous" groups like A.A. and therapeutic groups like Recovery, Inc., do not challenge the existent, predominantly middle-class or "mainstream" values of American society. By and large they accept these values and seek to assist their members to function more adequately in relation to them and within the conventional social framework. (Alcoholics Anonymous and its imitators also have strong religious biases and believe that religion, often an inherently conservative force, can assist individuals to accept and adapt to the prevailing social values.)

In contrast to such socially conforming groups there are a number that ostensibly and publicly reject all or some of the values of the dominant society. An example is Synanon, which in the past has rather frankly criticized the acquisitive elements in American society, the socially accepted values of middle-class marriage, family life, and morality, and so on. But Synanon's recent history shows that, while verbally opposing some values of the dominant society, it makes use of the possibilities of this society's economic structure and does not in actuality reject society's materialistic and acquisitive aspects. Thus, Synanon's real estate holdings and business ventures are well known; the monies realized from these prudent and profitable investments and undertakings are plowed back into the Synanon enterprise as a whole, for purposes of expansion, for further development of the program, and so forth. For these reasons, it is not accurate to speak of Synanon as rejecting "mainstream" values; rather, the organization seems to represent a variant form of expression, but one that is still consistent with the general ideas of the dominant American society and that presents no serious challenge to it.

There is, however, a third type of self-help group that openly challenges the values of the existing society. This type of group is exemplified by various radical protest bodies, as well as by some communes. If one takes a look at various protest movements built around opposition to war, such as the Movement for a Democratic Military (M.D.M.), the self-groupings of Vietnam veterans opposed to the war, and so on, one sees in them a clear challenge to the legalities and sanctions of government, to the rationale and methods of use of the powers of the state, its police, and so on.

There are, of course, wide variations among the hundreds of North American communes. Some communes have a strongly antiestablishment value structure; others have a specific radical or revolutionary political ideology; while still others are neutral on broader social and political questions, but represent a self-selected group of people devoted to a particular philosophy of life —Buddhism, meditation, drug usage, or group marriage, for example.

The small "consciousness-raising" groups in the Women's Liberation movement also have distinctive self-help characteristics. The radical element in the Women's Movement clearly rejects many of the prevailing values and ideologies of this society, which is perceived as male-oriented in the perpetuation of not only male dominance, sexism, and the subjugated status of women, but also in the most basic social institutions, such as property rights, individual enterprise, marriage, and the nuclear family.

All classifications—such as those advanced in this chapter—are tentative constructs, an aid to the understanding of complex realities; they are not to be thought of as existing in pure form. Each of the groups that we might assign to one or another of the types in our classification probably shares some elements of other definitions and classsifications. We hope that "primary focus," which we have stressed, will turn out to be a useful method of classifying the groups, but its limitations need to be borne in mind. That is why we take refuge in a residual category: "mixed" groups (see Chapter 8), whose characteristics do not fit exactly into any of the categories of our previous analysis.

In the following sections we have sought to illustrate each of the types of self-help groups in our fivefold classification scheme by presenting case studies—descriptive first-hand accounts or empirical studies—which in our view exemplify the main themes and characteristics of each variant form.

Before doing so, an explanation to readers of the manner of these presentations is in order.

We recognize that there is an inevitably wide variety of purposes, style, and approaches embodied in these illustrative "case studies," as there is in other reprinted or commissioned articles throughout this volume. Some of the selections are purely descriptive first-hand accounts and do not analyze or seek to generate theoretical ideas from the experiences they describe. Other writers approach their materials from divergent standpoints of social theory or social values. Despite their variegated presuppositions and framework, however, all the accounts we have selected throw light on the common theme we are examining: the intrinsic nature and distinguishable characteristics of peer "support systems."

In presenting these materials we have in most instances chosen to let the authors speak for themselves—our own comments on the selections usually follow rather than precede them; we prefer that readers first encounter these living materials as they came to us, without refraction through our own understanding of them.

5

Therapeutic
Type:
Recovery, Inc.

DONALD T. LEE

Accelerated releases of mental hospital patients have forced professionals to reconsider present methods of giving after-care services. Not only have more patients been released, but duration in the hospital is growing shorter. Inevitably, patients are returning to the community less handicapped socially by institutionalization. However, they may also have more residual symptoms. While the residual symptoms often are under some control through medication, these symptoms are a source of fear to the patient and alarm to the family because they are often precursors of rehospitalization.

Over thirty-one years ago, Recovery, Inc. was started by Dr. Abraham A. Low, a psychiatrist. His approach was designed to encourage his patients to carry out a self-help program that would permit them to control their symptoms. Today Recovery has 634 groups[1] and 10,000 to 12,000 people attending in the United States and Canada.*

We thought that such a program would be of use to our patients at Camarillo in helping them bridge the gap between the hospital and the community. The use of self-help organizations has become more widespread, [2,3] with some 265 different self-help groups identified nationally.[4]

Recovery, Inc., differing from other groups in being started by a psychiatrist, also more systematically integrates self-help as an active concept into its program. This attracted our attention as a necessary complement to present hospital-community treatment as well as to some of the following aspects.

This organization has a well-developed program of leadership training and supervision, weekly meetings are always held in public buildings available to all, patients may be referred by professionals or self-referred, and the meetings are open to inspection by anyone interested.

The meetings necessarily follow a structured format of introductions by first names, voluntary participation in reading from Dr. Low's book, four members presenting examples, "spotting" on the examples, a free will offering, then the question period for newcomers, and last, the period of mutual aid where individuals informally discuss Recovery methods. This later phase is often

SOURCE: Excerpted with permission from Donald T. Lee, A.C.S.W., *Mental Hygiene*, vol. 55, no. 2 (April 1971), pp. 194–197.

*The national headquarters of Recovery states that there were 942 groups in forty-six states and five provinces of Canada at the end of 1972. [Eds.]

carried on in some nearby coffee shop. The giving of examples is very important in showing how Recovery works. It follows four points: (1) a description of the event, who was there, and what was said; (2) the patient's description of his symptoms and his discomfort; (3) the patient's spotting of his temper and working-up process, and (4) how the patient would have reacted to this situation before his Recovery training. The examples are limited to five minutes and are concerned with "some triviality of everyday life."[5]

Basic Premises of Recovery

To better understand the panel examples and "spotting" it is necessary to examine four basic premises of Recovery.

The first is that although most patients returning home from a psychiatric hospital are greatly improved they still have "residual symptoms." These symptoms are usually described as various somatic manifestations or as "restlessness, tenseness, and preoccupation."[6] Low developed and modified this later in describing, "What they (the returning patients) are mostly afraid of are terrifying sensations, threatening impulses, obsessing thoughts and depressing feelings, that is, their own inner experiences."[7]

The second premise is the use of "Recovery Lingo." At Recovery meetings participants may not use psychiatric terms, analytic concepts, or religious or philosophical expressions.* In fact, only Recovery language is used. Dr. Low explained that this was to keep inexperienced people from straying into areas of complexes, childhood memories, dreams, and the like, but it also serves to keep the group's attention on those things they can do to exercise the self-help concept.[8]

The third is the very system of the Recovery method. In part this includes reading the book and attending meetings, but most of all it is the "spotting" process with its attending techniques for self-help. Here the word "spotting" is used in its meaning of "to note as suspicious; hence, to recognize, detect." In reading the book and attending meetings the patient is taught a number of

*Members may not discuss diagnosis, prognosis, or medication; nor may they recommend physicians.

Recovery concepts that he must recognize or detect in himself either as thoughts or behavior. This is spotting.

The fourth is self-endorsement. Each member is told that he must endorse himself (give himself praise) every time he makes the effort to use Recovery methods. He endorses the effort, not the success of his practice of the method.

Program at Camarillo State Hospital

The Recovery program held much promise as an additional resource for our patients leaving the hospital, and we thought that preparation in the hospital for attending groups in the community would promote better follow-through. Consequently, we secured permission from the National Headquarters of Recovery for carrying out a simulated Recovery program in the hospital. In keeping with the voluntary nature of Recovery we attempted to attract patients and avoided all semblances of having patients assigned to the group. Most patients reported later that they came because of the signs posted or because friends urged them to come. A few were referred by professionals.

The in-hospital meetings follow as nearly as possible the community Recovery meetings. The major difference is that the hospital groups have few if any experienced successful members to give depth in the Recovery method. The author has attempted to fill this role. More recently we have developed some patient leaders who have carried on meetings most effectively.

As a part of our program monthly evening meetings were conducted by a community group from Recovery, Inc. These meetings enabled present patients to meet former patients now practicing the Recovery method to maintain their mental health. Meeting others who have made constructive changes in their own lives affords the hospital patient a more hopeful experience. It also gives patients the chance to meet and know some of the leaders and members of the groups in the community and helps to allay uncertainties patients may have in entering new situations.

In the Los Angeles area there are more than fifty groups holding weekly meetings. Almost every area is within easy access. A booklet published by the hospital of the meeting places, indexed by date and location, is given to all interested patients. Every meeting in the hospital includes a period for discussing the location of community meetings, and patients are encouraged to attend as soon as they leave the hospital.

Evaluation

This report spans the first sixteen months of our Recovery program (February 1967–May 1968). (Three and a half years later there has been no significant change in the types of patients attending as revealed in the data reported.) There were 121 meetings held with a total attendance of 394, of which 364 are being reported on. The average attendance was 11.6 patients per meeting. There were ten meetings with between 20 and 32 patients, but these large groups are very difficult to conduct and were not encouraged, as too many patients unfamiliar with Recovery impede the program.

The median times attended was two, while 62.9 percent (229) attended one or two times and 37.1 percent (135) attended three to fifty-one times. In many instances patients attended just prior to leaving the hospital and were only available one or two times. Almost three-fourths (74.2 percent) of the patients who attended had been admitted during the same sixteen-month period covered by these meetings. Most attended within a few weeks after their admission. Patients in the hospital for a year accounted for 10.7 percent of attendance, while 13.5 percent had been in the hospital from two to twenty years. (Admission data are unknown for 1.6 percent.) Among all the patients attending, 53.2 percent were committed and the remainder were voluntary (46.8 percent). This corresponds closely to the almost equal numbers of committed and voluntary patients admitted over the past several years.

This group did attract a disproportionate share of women patients. In admissions to Camarillo, 49.4 percent are women,[9] while 61.4 percent of those attending our group were women. Ethnic differences were most notable, with the preponderance being white (94.0 percent). Negroes account for 8.7 percent of admissions to California hospitals,[10] but 5.2 percent came to Recovery. Other minorities were even more poorly represented, accounting for 4.3 percent of admissions,[11] but only 0.8 percent came to our group.

Attention should be called to the large number of schizophrenic patients (53.6 percent) who seek out Recovery. The percentage of schizophrenics among first admissions is 27.2 percent. Patients with psychotic depressions (12.1 percent) came disproportionately compared with first admissions (7.4 percent). This is further accentuated, with depressive reactions predominating among patients diagnosed as psychoneurotic (13.7 percent). Under-representation was found among patients with chronic brain syndrome and personality disorder diagnoses.

There were marked differences between men and women attending Recovery meetings, with older women and younger men predominating. The median age for all patients was 37.7 years, which corresponds with 38.8 years for first-admission patients statewide.[1] However, the median age for men in our group was 33.0 years and for women 40.8 years.

There were many more single men (51.4 percent) than single women (24.1 percent) in the Recovery group and more divorced women (29.0 percent) than divorced men (23.6 percent).

Protestants predominated with 55.5 percent in the Recovery group versus the United States Census figure of 66.1 percent.[12] There were 23.3 percent Catholic patients attending versus United States Census of 25.7 percent.[13] The census shows 3.3 percent of U.S. population Jewish,[14] while our group had 12.5 percent in this category.

Since Recovery is a highly verbally oriented program, educational level might be expected to play a significant role in the self-selection process. This is borne out by our findings that more patients had partial college or completed college (28.6 percent), while 25.8 percent had less than high school education. There were also more high school graduates in the Recovery group (35.2 percent) than among statewide patients (24.4 percent).[15]

Conclusions

The Recovery method is important not only as a self-help system for patients, but because it offers significant conceptualizations for the use of professionals[16] in their own work with patients. It tends to create a "well role model" for patients to follow in the crucial area of interpersonal relationships.[17] Because the Recovery program is so widespread it offers help to patients and their families during the critical after-care period immediately following release.[18] The program is flexible and supports other therapeutic efforts being undertaken by professionals.

The self-help aspects are important in maintaining or restoring dignity to individuals who may have lost it in the process of becoming a mental patient. The Recovery method holds out a goal for members that can be shared by many professionals. This goal, expressed with warm humor by some experienced old-timer, is that you aspire to stop being a nervous patient and just become a nervous person.

A placid poor get nothing, but a turbulent
poor sometimes gets something.
—Frances Fox Piven and
Richard A. Cloward

6

Social Advocacy Type: The National Welfare Rights Organization
FRANCES FOX PIVEN
and
RICHARD A. CLOWARD

In the 1960's, as in the 1930's, poor people banded together to attack the relief system. Just as unemployed groups sprang up during the Depression and eventually banded together in the Workers' Alliance, so in the late 1960's welfare rights groups began to appear and then banded together in a National Welfare Rights Organization. In some respects these organizations bear little similarity to each other: the Alliance was composed primarily of unemployed white men, whereas NWRO is composed mostly of black women who are, practically speaking, unemployable in today's market. But there are also striking similarities: each arose in a period of widespread social and political upheaval occasioned by profound economic dislocation, and each flourished by capitalizing on disorder to obtain public aid for masses of families in financial distress.

The first welfare protest groups originated in the OEO [Office of Economic Opportunity] agencies. But once such groups came into being, so did the possibility of building a national grass-roots organization through relief protests. Some independent activists came to see this. Their interest was stimulated by a paper we circulated in late 1965 among anti-poverty workers, organizers, and activists entitled "Mobilizing the Poor: How It Can Be Done." It called upon those who were working with welfare recipients, as well as other activists, to form a movement with the express purpose of getting hundreds of thousands of families onto the relief rolls, for we had by then conducted sufficient research to establish that only half of the eligible poor were on the rolls. To deal with these problems, we argued, mayors and governors would call upon the federal government with increasing insistency to establish a federally financed minimum income.

The most important activist to see these possibilities was Dr. George A. Wiley, a professor of chemistry who had joined the civil rights movement and become the associate national director of CORE [Congress of Racial Equality]. In the late spring of 1966 he left CORE to open the Poverty/Rights Action Center in Washington, D.C. Within several months, PRAC became the organizing vehicle for what was to become the National Welfare Rights Organization; and under Wiley's leadership, the organization has since burgeoned.

SOURCE: Excerpted with permission from Frances Fox Piven and Richard A. Cloward, "How the Federal Government Caused the Welfare Crisis," *Social Policy*, May–June 1971.

Wiley, with Edwin Day and later Timothy Sampson, began by making strenuous efforts to establish links with the scattered welfare groups that already existed around the country and to spur the staff of anti-poverty agencies (as well as activists who were in limbo after the civil rights movement passed its peak) to concentrate on organizing in the field of welfare. The idea spread rapidly, especially among anti-poverty staff. As new groups developed, Wiley established contact and urged them to affiliate with the national headquarters. In February 1967, 350 leaders representing 200 welfare groups in 70 cities of 26 states answered the call to attend the first national meeting. Participating groups ranged from Mothers of Watts to Mothers for Adequate Welfare in Boston; from Chicago's Welfare Union of the West Side Organization, composed of unemployed black men, to eastern Kentucky's Committee to Save Unemployed Fathers, consisting of unemployed white miners. Most of the groups originated in anti-poverty agencies, but some had been organized by churchmen, others by civil rights activists, and still others by Students for a Democratic Society. By 1969 NWRO claimed more than 100,000 dues-paying members in some 350 local groups.

The new organization first came to national attention in June 1966. On June 20, Reverend Paul Younger and Edith Doering, welfare rights organizers who had been hired by the Cleveland Council of Churches, led about 40 welfare recipients out of Cleveland on the first lap of a 155-mile march to Columbus to lobby with the governor for an increase in Ohio's welfare payments. On the morning of June 30, when they finally reached Columbus, the 40 marchers were joined by 2,000 recipients and sympathizers from other towns in Ohio. On the same day in New York, 2,000 recipients massed in front of City Hall. Groups of recipients in 15 other cities, including Baltimore, Washington, Los Angeles, Boston, Louisville, Chicago, Trenton, and San Francisco, also joined demonstrations against "the welfare."

By now NWRO is fairly well known, especially in northern cities, where local groups have staged hundreds of demonstrations to protest various welfare restrictions. Thousands of welfare recipients and organizers have been jailed on charges from trespass to riot. In the South, storefront offices have been razed, and welfare rights leaders' homes have been burned. This past winter and spring NWRO led a campaign to reinstate thousands of families who were abruptly cut off the rolls in Nevada.

Most organizing across the nation has consisted of efforts to settle individual grievances. . . .

Welfare rights groups have also mounted large-scale campaigns to obtain certain benefits that many people are entitled to but few receive. As we have observed earlier, for example, many welfare departments officially permit extra grants for special purposes, but people are rarely told about them and generally don't get them. Staging a "mass benefit campaign" requires less organizing effort than the laborious process of adjusting individual grievances and produces a far greater financial payoff. School clothing lists, for example, are mimeographed and widely distributed in slum neighborhoods, together with an announcement of a forthcoming demonstration at the welfare center. When hundreds of people assemble with a common demand, welfare departments usually release the grants, especially in cities where public officials fear that repression will provoke outbreaks of violence in the ghettos.

Campaigns of this sort in New York City included week-long sit-ins and forced some district welfare centers to close down. As the system lost control over its discretionary giving, the costs of special grants zoomed from about $40 per recipient in 1965 to $100 in 1968. When the aggregate costs reached an annual rate of $100 million, *The New York Times* was moved editorially to call these campaigns a "threat to (New York City's) treasury." To blunt that threat, state officials—responding to increased white antagonism toward welfare costs—abolished the special grant. But in the meantime, a great many people had got a great deal of money that they would not otherwise have received.

These campaigns were greatly aided by the contagious effects of successful welfare rights activity. In May 1968, for example, thousands of Puerto Rican mothers and children who were not affiliated with NWRO unexpectedly appeared in the South Bronx relief centers demanding money. After long sit-ins, checks were disbursed. Relief administrations attributed this avalanche of requests to a clothing grants campaign being conducted at the time by the City-Wide Coordinating Council of Welfare Groups. But they were wrong. The relief offices were engulfed by this mass of people, it turned out, because a rumor of unknown origin had spread to the effect that a wealthy patron had died and left $50 million to the welfare department to be given to the poor. Nor could the rumor be dispelled. Within days, it spread to Spanish Harlem and then to Central Harlem, and the relief offices in those districts were flooded, forcing the check-writing machines into a virtual twenty-four-hour schedule. These unplanned demonstrations were partly responsible for the fact that the cost of special grants, which had totaled some $3 million in the same month a year earlier, reached $13 million in June 1968. For, except by calling the police and thus risking mass violence, how else was the welfare department to clear its offices and restore control? . . .

NWRO's organizing activities, it should be pointed out, were conducted mainly to benefit people already on the welfare rolls, for NWRO is an organization composed of recipients. To keep their members interested and involved, NWRO organizers have been constantly under pressure to increase benefits for existing recipients rather than to find and organize the nonrecipient poor for the purpose of getting them on the rolls. For this reason, NWRO's contribution to the rising welfare rolls has been slum and ghetto families who witness demonstrations over grievances and demands for special grants or for higher grants and become more aware of their own rights and less fearful of applying for aid. . . .

If NWRO developed as a by-product of federal intervention in the cities, it later came to have quite direct relations with the national government. In 1968 the outgoing Johnson administration granted NWRO more than $400,000 through the Department of Labor, a sum roughly equivalent to the total amount raised from private sources after the organization formed in early 1966. The money was ostensibly to be used to monitor the local employment programs for AFDC [Aid to Families with Dependent Children] mothers, which had been mandated by the congressional amendments of 1967 in order to ensure that participation in training would be fully voluntary. However, federal officials were aware that a substantial part of the money would go toward strengthening local relief groups. The fact that the national government openly financed an organization of America's poor that was harassing local welfare departments is dramatic evidence of the federal role in the welfare explosion in the late 1960's.

Bob Henderson robs banks. And teaches Al Breau to read and write. And assures Garry that medication for his epilepsy is necessary and really nobody looks sideways at him for it. In Bob Henderson, nine years left on his parole, kindness and generosity abound. His peculiar beacon is Patience. (Who else knows this virtue today?)

7

"Rock-Bottom Haven" Type: X-Kalay

DAVID M. BERNER and LEWIS MOLINA

The real significance of X-Kalay has little to do with the peculiarities of its resident employees: ex-drug addicts, alcoholics, thieves, prostitutes, unwed mothers and fathers

and hung-up university dropouts. In our formative years the glue
holding us together was adversity. The mold was shaped and
solidified time and again, through recurring crises by the collective sorrow of our members, our family.

Can you sell cars and not crank up, John?

*Will you run back to that sot or find another one just like him,
Sally?*

*Do you really know anyone else in this damn town who cares
enough to pick you up, kick your ass, wipe your nose when
you're too fucking lazy or stupid to do it yourself?*

The real significance of X-Kalay has everything to do with the
fact that 110 variously sad and inspired men, women, and children live together. We believe we have found ways to be together
not only successfully, but happily with surging creativity.

X-Kalay is identified by some observers as a rigorous and demanding proponent of discipline, a milieu that permits no passing
of the behavioral buck. We are also viewed as firm and often
scolding parents who insist upon nothing but the best and are
intolerant of the art of blamesmanship. To others we seem a
madhouse, an eccentric commune of crazies, encouraging the
most outrageous fancies of our residents to burst forth at unpre-
dictable times and places. . . .

In truth both attitudes prevail here. How can it be justified?
Are we organizers or freak-outs? Do we want (and practice) an-
archy, democratic order, or tyranny? Let's put it this way: We
are a riotous matching of wits and monumental demands made on
each other, a pouring forth of gut debris, culminating in a collective answer to our collective problems.

The Beginnings

I (DMB) am thirty-one years old, born in Winnipeg and the
founder and executive director of the X-Kalay Foundation. Lew
Molina is an ex-Californian, a member of our board of directors,
and oversees our Winnipeg operation.

I grew up, it seems like most Jewish kids, in the North End of
Winnipeg—in a pool hall. Not only Winnipeg's Jews, but Poles,

Ukrainians, Hungarians, and everybody from anywhere lived in that part of town; there was a good, solid yarmulke-wearing feeling permeating the North Star Pool Hall.

By sixteen I had devoured James Joyce and Henry Miller and fancied myself a writer. Being a "writer" but also a restless kid, I joined the Canadian Air Force. A year later and the Air Force experience behind me, I landed a job as a schoolteacher in Lac du Bonnie, Manitoba. I lasted for five months. One day I looked at my class, decided the whole thing was a waste of time, walked out the door, and took myself off to Europe.

I returned from Europe and enrolled for a couple of years in a university, left that and went to the temperate climate of British Columbia. To the casual onlooker I probably revealed the obvious symptoms of "sociosis." Marijuana, liquor, saxophone blowing jazz in a house on Burrard Street at 3 A.M. Taxi driving to the tune of "Pulse, Pulse," in downtown Vancouver with its executives and its ordinary whores and its executive whores. I flipped out a bit. But fortunately for myself and perhaps for the lives of hundreds of people, as well, I landed right side up.

The Bungalow on Fifth Avenue

In January 1967 I found myself on the staff of the Company of Young Canadians (the equivalent on a far smaller scale of VISTA, the U.S. Urban Peace Corps). What the CYC offered me was a chance to go to Ottawa for training—nothing more. . . . About that time, however, a group of Canadian Indians at the British Columbia Penitentiary formed the Indian Educational Club and asked me to help them in starting a halfway house for paroled inmates. On January 29, 1967, two ex-cons and I emptied our pockets and pooled the sum of $137. That inconspicuous event began what is today the X-Kalay Foundation, an organization that has reversed the path of some of Canada's most hopeless and "incurable" social lepers.

X-Kalay, identified in 1967 as the Indian Post-Release Center Society, had its inception in a bungalow on Fifth Avenue in Point Grey, Vancouver.

Nobody among us really knew what was happening or could happen. There was only a dream, an idea that somehow there must be an alternative to the cycle of drunk-arrest-jail-release-drunk-jail facing so many of Canada's first- and second-class citizens. But there were no formulas and no panaceas.

Guys wandered in, mostly from the Pen but sometimes from The Street, and stayed there for a while. While a man was at the Post-Release Center, he worked if he could, didn't if he couldn't, and generally hung around to get it all together before taking the big plunge into the Straight World. Liquor was then permitted on the premises and some guys used drugs, and occasionally there was a fight that raised hell with both our regular and informal programs. Meanwhile I was trying to get these fellows to jobs that I had scrounged up for them. Very slowly it began to work. By January 1968 we were able to obtain a loan of $5,000 from the Vancouver Kiwanis Club, and we bought a house for the group.

It wasn't much of a house; paint was rotting when you could find it, and grease coated the kitchen. But the guys set to work cleaning and scraping and soon it was comfortable. Our people still went out to jobs, both regular and intermittent, but not without being hounded, cajoled, and literally driven to their work-places day and night by our staff. But our house members and visitors still drank and used drugs. This finally came to a halt in February 1968 when through group decision liquor and drugs were forbidden on the premises. The solution for a determined lush though was simple: go off the property to become plastered. In response to this the Foundation soon insisted upon two *immutable* rules, which have been continually enforced and are still operative:

1|No use of any mood-changing drugs, including alcohol, by any member at any time or place.

2|No threats or use of violence at any time or place.

Socializing the New Member

Since X-Kalay is a realistic social-interactional community, *it deals with the entire spectrum of personal and social development.* Upon becoming a resident a new member's prior personal sense of authority and self-concept, usually built upon quicksand, is quickly *minimized* through our unrelenting social pressures. Dependency is induced and the novitiate is manipulated or maneuvered into a variety of situations that are designed to force him to come to terms with his personal inadequacies in the real world. Gradually, over a period of months, the pressures inducing dependency are reduced. Upward mobility within the Foundation's social system is encouraged. Necessities are provided for every member, but the more an individual demonstrates personal initiative and responsibility the greater his access to whatever amenities exist within the facility. In practical terms, the member carrying responsibility for a crew or "Tribe" may have an automobile available to him, whereas a new member of low status does not. Such dependent status is typically transformed into an independent one in the sense that the resident, after a period of time, may see himself as a *provider for* the Foundation. Thus he may work in an outside business that is financially productive, yet his status with us is contingent upon the success of his efforts here. No member of X-Kalay is salaried; all profits accruing from X-Kalay support the collective Foundation.

Socialization demands are intense and the environment presents difficulties for a new entrant. With no recognition given for the previous deviant status held by the newcomer, the former criminal or drug user cannot have a "solid identity." His choices are clear—and limited: (1) *retain personality and social characteristics that are acceptable in the counter-culture or deviant subcultures and be ostracized in X-Kalay* or (2) *adopt a traditional, middle-class and socially appropriate set of personal and group behaviors and obtain positive recognition within the Foundation.*

If an individual can cope with the prescriptions for personal change embodied in the overall challenge of X-Kalay, chances are that a more realistic and healthy human being will emerge. Along with an increasing security of self and a parallel authority earned via socially desirable behaviors, we have observed the growth of both *a relevant personal morality and a social consciousness.* This extends from concern only with one's self to a sense of what it means to be a Canadian citizen in the 1970's—to what it takes to be an interacting human being in a very complex world.

At this point, and armed with job skills acquired at the Foundation, the veteran member is faced with a decision: either leave X-Kalay as a "rehabilitated" person ready to enter the Canadian mainstream or stay in X-Kalay and contribute to its primary and secondary concerns—people and business enterprises.

The Tribe
Even in a relatively small organization a new member can feel lost and impersonalized, particularly if he enters with a weak self-image. In a small group he learns more rapidly whom he has to relate to and whom he is responsible to and for what reasons. Not long ago we divided the resident population into small groups of ten to fifteen, called Tribes. Each Tribe is directed by a role-modeling senior employee of the Foundation. Tribe members have the opportunity to plan for and participate via their group in such activities as a monthly newspaper, weekly newsletters, daily educational seminars, drama workshops, athletics, and much simple hard work around the facility. The Tribe arrangement is also viewed as a useful counterpart of the "Game," that is an informal, pressure-reducing ministructure.

Core Therapy
The Game, a unique form of social encounter, is the core therapeutic process of X-Kalay. Games are vehicles for group encounters and are played three nights a week. A variety of psychotherapeutic techniques come into play without professional helpers in order to maximize the emotional growth of the participants. By now it has become a sophisticated potpourri of methods of relating. When Games were first begun they resembled nothing so much as screaming battles extending for hours. However, no one was ever assaulted during these encounters or afterward. The members, newcomers and old-timers alike, called each other the worst names in the book, yet nobody ever took a swing at anybody else. Furthermore, very few people split from our premises because of the Game. Many of the residents, it should be noted, had been, just a short time before, knife-wielding, heroin-taking toughs of the most violent sort. We credit the Game with helping these people learn other ways of expressing anger and frustration through techniques of Gestalt, Reality, and

Psychodrama therapies. But the key to the effectiveness of the Game rests with X-Kalay's whole milieu: combining work, play, and learning for its residents in a continuously social way.

Business Ventures

At an early stage of our development we entered the world of business by taking over a lease on a service station. We thought our people should have pride of business ownership and learn how to deal with outsiders in the real world. The experience lasted all of two days. We had to chalk up that failure to lack of experience and know-how.

In August 1969 the Foundation, then numbering about twenty men, women, and one child, purchased a house in Lower Shaugnessey in Vancouver. We were able to afford the down payment through the sale of our previous house.

Now an old slum house on Fifth Avenue is one thing, but X-Kalay in Lower Shaugnessey? The neighbors were outraged. These were ex-convicts, they said, and besides they were *Indians* and *unmarried men* and *women*. By now, used to this kind of hypocrisy, the Foundation took on the neighbors at City Council hearings and won the right to remain.

We tried again with a gas station and this time it worked. The Foundation began leasing and successfully operating a service station on West Broadway. The guys who worked there, pumping gas and making change, were the same group who used to rob service stations. X-Kalay was finally in business and all profits went back into our coffers for food, clothing, and shelter. No one in X-Kalay receives a salary of any kind. (In my capacity as executive director, I and my family receive a living allowance.)

Then there was Seton Academy, a former convent and school. If you drive to the top of the North Burnaby Hills in Vancouver, you see an outstanding piece of property. X-Kalay could easily house 100 men, women, and children on the site and there were six classrooms for immediate use. Moreover, the academy was for sale. But the nearby neighbors of the academy didn't quite see it the same way. Ex-cons and former drug addicts. . . . So the battle commenced. Petitions, newspaper editorials, radio, TV, the works. We had managed to talk the Canadian Mortgage &

Homeloan Corporation into footing the mortgage and had scrounged the 10 percent down, but Burnaby City Council approval was needed. There ensued a zoning hearing, which still holds the attendance record in Burnaby, almost 1,000 people. X-Kalay lost when the City Council, on a technicality, decided not to vote on this issue. The Foundation took the case to the British Columbia Supreme Court and lost again. (Chalk it up again to experience.)

In March 1970 the Foundation numbered about 40 men, women, and children. Approximately 150 people had come in, stayed awhile and left. The recidivism rate, residents who had been returned to jail, was about 15 percent. That's the lowest anywhere in Canada.

X-Kalay had also started a second business called the B.C. Pen Company, which sold ball-point pen imprinting to commercial firms. Forty people, no drugs, no booze or violence, two businesses, and at the same time running a federal-government-sponsored program at Matsqui Institution for drug offenders. We soon realized that the Shaugnessey house was far too small to encompass both the people and programs envisioned in the future.

The next step was to rent a warehouse—10,000 square feet of scrap lumber, old useless sheet metal, and crud. We wanted to turn it into our headquarters and make it a palace. We did. . . .

A few Vancouver businessmen, our faithful sponsors, donated all kinds of materials. Some 25,000 square feet of gyprock for construction of seminar rooms, lounges, and offices. Some hundreds of feet of flourescent lighting, as well as several thousand dollars in direct financial contributions. And the residents of X-Kalay worked their butts off making a home for themselves. Former bank robbers became electricians and formerly disgruntled pill-popping store clerks became carpenters.

Since August 1970 X-Kalay's growth has been phenomenal. Next there was another business, X-Kalay Hair, a beauty salon in the Oakridge section of Vancouver, a stable, middle-class area. Then we acquired a satellite installation in British Columbia, an old and beautiful resort hotel featuring a dining room and coffee shop on Salt Spring Island. And finally, the big one, a new site in Winnipeg, 1,500 miles eastward.

Geographical Expansion

The X-Kalay directors submitted a brief to the Manitoba Government in November 1970 proposing a facility in that province. The Provincial Government agreed and on June 15, 1971, gave the Foundation an establishing grant of $7,000. On June 24 four residents arrived in Winnipeg and on July 5 the X-Kalay Foundation of Manitoba, Inc., was formed.

Within six months a great many things had been accomplished. We situated more than forty people, including families, on a huge primary facility and physical plant (a former convent) on 80 acres in St. Norbert, a suburb of Winnipeg. We initiated two projects: the X-Kalay Advertising Specialities Company and the X-Kalay Drop-In & Counseling Centre. Of importance too was our opening of the Lyceum—the first parent-cooperative community to be launched in the entire province. Concurrently we began to operate programs at the Headingly Correctional Institution, the Stony Mountain Penitentiary, and Selkirk Mental Hospital. (Anyone for community development?)

Problems and Issues: The "Unknown Path" Takes Shape

The X-Kalay Foundation celebrated its fifth anniversary on January 29, 1972. We felt proud of the fact that the X-Kalay scene has been a changing one, reflecting our collective excitement over new ways of serving our own membership as well as the larger community. We have drawn up plans to unite all our residents under one roof in the near future. A distinguished Canadian architectural firm, Erickson-Massey, designers of the Canadian Pavilion in Osaka in 1967, the Montreal Expo in 1967, and Simon Fraser University, has agreed to design a minivillage on a 4-acre site overlooking the Fraser River in Vancouver.

Since its inception, our scope of operations has been expanding. But it was time to call a halt, a sort of moratorium on growth, with a view toward consolidation. A number of decisions were taken regarding the optimal size of the various installations. The Vancouver facility was to be limited to 40, the Salt Springs operation to 20, and Winnipeg–St. Norbert to 80.

The expansion model made us aware of a fundamental value choice that lay before us. It had seemed we were destined to be businessmen and people-oriented at the same time. This brought up a conflict of personal style and public role, which we wished to either avoid or minimize in the future. Further expansion is not ruled out, as long as public and/or private funding sources remain willing to underwrite our endeavors. However, in giving us support, government bureaus, agencies, foundations, etc., must also be prepared to abide by two conditions:

1|The entire sum of the grant is to be provided by the granting agency. At this time we won't consider any formulas for matching grants.

2|The granting agency is to employ a professional money management expert and assign him to our Foundation. That person would be given an office within one of our facilities and would oversee grant expenditures and the accompanying paperwork.

Realistically this means at least for one year or two plans will be laid aside with respect to developing new facilities in Ottawa, the national capital; Regina, Saskatchewan, a provincial capital; and Toronto. Our newer approach is based on an assessment and a reaction to Synanon's experiences. The Synanon leadership has opted for a steady increase of their resident populations, thereby making it necessary to seek out further business activities and to acquire more land and housing. *In our view, business values as exemplified in Synanon's outlook could well drive out the values of humanized personal interactions.*

There are internal consequences too of such a policy. Residents can be told "you don't have to be here forever," and members can leave the Foundation without an accompanying sense of guilt. There are other possibilities. Members can more readily contribute at their own level on the basis of prearranged negotiating and contracting for tasks they wish to undertake upon being accepted as residents. A new tradition is henceforth to be developed called *graduating.* It resembles a rites-of-passage ceremony in order to help an individual make a clean break from the Foundation into the larger society. It is hoped that the ex-resident will feel free to come back to X-Kalay when he wants to. This means to us that he would be encouraged to participate in the gamut of

Foundation in-house programs as well as its community service endeavors, rather than be forced to polarize his identity as an "ex" rather than a real member. If this process is successful, it will acknowledge in a positive way what has actually been going on for some time, that is the great variety of actual role-repertoires available to the three subgroups associated with X-Kalay:

1|*The Regulars* who are resident in and employed internally by X-Kalay.

2|*The Careerists* who live in but work externally, either in a Foundation-sponsored activity or a job they themselves have located.

3|*The Life Stylers*. These are usually employed in law, social work, business, etc., and who move in lock, stock, and barrel, while retaining their outside positions. They too contribute their entire salary to X-Kalay.

Many residents feel that Life Stylers should comprise no more than 10 percent of the membership; it is alleged that their articulateness and drive tends to overwhelm the rest of the residents. Moreover, their middle-class style of dress and their comportment make it difficult for the others.

Public relations remains a day-to-day issue. X-Kalay does not specifically seek out drug addicts. Instead, we also look for new members among ex-cons, alcoholics, skid-row types, and people generally at loose ends. Yet our P.R. image seems to consist of a membership composed exclusively of ex-drug addicts.

We are currently evaluating our entire approach to the Game. Too often in the past we have mistaken gut-level emotionalism for purposeful and responsible behavior within our organization. We are now emphasizing a *rational* approach whereby individuals are judged more on what they contribute to the Foundation and to their growth than on the degree to which they merely articulate insights in playing the Synanon-derived game. Our motto—*Character is the only rank*—should become even more meaningful in the future. But the primary responsibility in the foreseeable future for a redirection of program goals and style of personal interaction will continue to rest initially with the executive director and his key aides. We feel we must continue to be effective role models to expedite these changes.

It is clear from the foregoing account that while adapting to Canadian conditions and lacking Synanon's proselytizing-expansionist zeal, X-Kalay shares some philosophical and structural features with the better-known organization. We had intended to include two articles presenting a wholly supportive and an analytically critical view of Synanon. Space limitations and the fact that Synanon is probably the most widely reported, self-help group counseled their omission.

The following listing, however, summarizes the positive and negative characterizations of Synanon appearing in the representative articles by Enright and Collier that we had hoped to include.

Enright—positive[1]

- not a treatment, but an opportunity
- a real social movement
- non-medical model therapy
- an exciting place to live
- philosophical openness
- self-reliance
- experiential learning
- many role models
- no "professional-client" relationship
- truth-seeking through games
- commercial expansion and "hustling" necessary and justified
- game techniques work well
- responsible behavior insisted upon

Collier—negative[2]

- a substitute for realistic processes of treatment
- deals with individuals easily molded
- too institutionalized to be a social movement
- "Stalinist" and regimented
- brainwashing
- dogma and church-like
- one role model, e.g., Charles Dederich
- sadism through games/self-flagellation
- commercial expansion and hustling have unfortunate side effects
- game techniques have some questionable consequences
- such responsibility symbolized totalitarianism

8

Some Mixed Forms of Self-Help Groups

A number of self-help groups, such as Parents Without Partners, the Seventh Step, and the Fortune Society, as well as other organizations of ex-prisoners, do not fit neatly into one of the categories of the fourfold classification scheme presented in Chapter 4. They have a "mixed" character, showing some element of several categories but without a strong or dominant focus. In this chapter we describe and analyze some groups of this nature both because of the importance and pervasiveness of the social problems with which they deal and because they represent a numerically and substantively significant variant form.

The primary focus of these groups is not on personal growth, as in the "therapeutic" groups; *or* on social advocacy, *or* on the creation of alternative living patterns. Nor do they represent what we have termed "outcast haven" or "rock-bottom" groups. Instead, they have been organized to meet the specific and personalized set of problems their members confront; in Parents without Partners the difficulties of raising children as a single parent; in the many burgeoning ex-prisoner groups, everything related to the stigma of being a former felon—the difficulties of getting a job, housing, resocialization, acceptance, and so on.

Typically, these mixed groups do not have a worked-out ideology and codified procedures for the rehabilitation or socialization of their members as do A.A. (Alcoholics Anonymous) and other "anonymous" groups. They do not engage in consciously or specifically "therapeutic" activities as found in the meetings of Recovery, Inc., or the Synanon Game. Nor are they—at least initially—cause- or social action-oriented, and they usually do not call or work for a radical reconstruction of society. Instead, they concentrate on organizing material benefits and educational and social activities for their members, with the objective of enhancing the social competence and coping ability of their members to meet the socially stressful situations they share.

Parents Without Partners

Parents Without Partners illustrates some of the characteristics and limitations of this type of group.

PWP seems largely middle class in membership outlook, and its psychological orientation reflects the concerns of a group that does not reject the dominant social values but, rather, seeks greater self-understanding through varieties of psychotherapy.

Typically, the main activity of its chapters is to present lectures or hold discussions on child-rearing, the special problems of divorced women and men, dating, and so on.

As Elizabeth Harris observes: "The primary purpose of PWP is educational. Its members tend to be psychiatrically sophisticated, and members of the ortho-psychiatric disciplines are popular as speakers and discussion leaders. . . . While some chapters designate their professionally led discussion programs as 'group therapy,' this is an inaccurate euphemism. Such groups tend to remain—and probably should remain—on the level of family life education workshops."[1]

Clearly, PWP is meeting a widespread need, as witnessed by its rapid growth since its founding in 1957 to more than 200 chapters, with some 30,000 members. The organization appeals to many people—particularly to women, since, perhaps because of custody practices in divorce proceedings, they outnumber men in its membership by three to one.[2] PWP members probably join the organization for a variety of reasons—some for purely social reasons, that is, companionship, to meet new prospective partners; others to obtain information pertinent to their situation.

In contrast to personal growth groups, PWP does not seem to carry out searching and meaningful group discussions of the problems many members have in common as single parents. The "consciousness-raising" techniques of the Women's Movement, described in Part V, would seem to be ideally adapted to the needs of PWP members, since the basis of that method is to help members realize the relationship of personal to social problems, define and deal with their feelings about men, their sexuality, the institution of marriage, sex discrimination, and related topics.

PWP has not seemed to want to travel that path, which could lead to the questioning of many basic social values. Indeed, the very name Parents WITHOUT Partners seems to imply an initial acceptance of the stigma of an inferior position; the belief is that "parents WITH partners"—in keeping with the prevailing social norm—are better.[3] Implicitly accepting these ideas, PWP tries to help its members cope with their lot through psychotherapy and self-understanding. Its goals would seem to be its members' short-term survival from the traumas of family breakup and wid-

owhood and support in helping them get back into the competi-
tive social/sexual rat race of dating and remarriage.

So, PWP, in general, poses no criticism of the society or its
values, but, implicitly, does castigate individuals who have not
"made it," according to prevailing standards. It is thus a short
step for PWP members to internalize these "failures" at the marriage game, to emerge with a poor view of themselves, as mir-
rored in society's stigmatization of "single" parents, and to seek
to change that condition as soon as possible.

The contrast between the viewpoint of PWP and many of the
radical sections of the Women's Movement is well-expressed in
the words of Heather Booth: "You know, that's how you become
a radical—when you realize a problem is societal and not individual. . . . When you start fighting your own battles."

This ideological conflict is well illustrated by some recent history of single-parent groups in western Canada. In Calgary, a city
of 440,000, three groups of single parents were in existence in
early 1973. PWP Calgary, a local and unaffiliated association, was
initiated in 1962 by the local YM-YWCA and supported by the
Calgary Family Service Agency. The highlights of its program are
social: monthly membership meetings, bi-weekly dances, Christ-
mas and Easter parties, and a Halloween celebration for members' children. Membership is approximately 60 percent female
and 40 percent male. Attendance at monthly meetings ranges
from 20 to 75, with 25 to 40 a more typical gathering. A smaller
group, Minus One, has a similar program but without ties to
social service agencies.

PWP, Inc., a chapter of PWP International, was organized in
1970 and is the most recent entry into the single-parent field. It
was started because PWP Calgary had grown to 380 members,
too large for effective interpersonal interactions. PWP, Inc., also
wished to place less emphasis upon educational and social affairs
and more on recreational programs involving members' children.

Among these three groups a numerically small but significant
minority sought to connect larger social issues and problems to
the members' personal problems. For the most part, female students at the local junior college and the University of Calgary
were more responsive to the ideology of the counter-culture and

Women's Liberation than other members. Some had had contact with the public welfare system; they saw themselves as "welfare mothers" and maintained an interest concurrently in the Calgary Welfare Rights Organization.

This minority group of members of all three organizations continues to strive to bring about more concern and political activity within the organizations on single women's problems of employment, housing, child care, and welfare, in addition to a more radical approach to the personal problems of sexuality, marriage, and self-fulfillment. The strains and contradictions inherent in the life-style and ideological conflicts could well result in further schisms.

Ex-Prisoner Groups

One of the prominent ex-prisoner groups, Seventh Step, also has limited and relatively short-term goals for its members, even though their problems are severe and profound.

Seventh Step activities seem aimed first at meeting its members' concrete problems of living—especially, jobs; second, the reestablishment of social ties, housing, and so on. Only minor and sporadic attention is given to questions of civil rights and the social position of the ex-convict. Individual Seventh Step chapters have different points of program emphasis, but most center on the daily living problems of their members.

But here, Seventh Step, like other ex-prisoners' groups, confronts a dilemma. The establishment of basic trust in one another is a precondition for an organization to work effectively and to grow. For ex-convicts, the freedom to express themselves has been so curbed by society that it is very hard for them to trust each other individually, let alone in a group. Each ex-convict has already been negatively defined in strong terms by society and by other ex-cons as well. So it is a particularly difficult task to establish or find trust in an organization, despite the common bond of being negatively defined by the outside world.

Any group of people who share the same problems, ex-cons as well as other self-help group members, can get understanding and support from one another. But the way society's definition of the problem is perceived and dealt with by that group is crucial for the individual member. If one is stigmatized as a social deviant, an "ex-con" or a "dope addict," there are two alternatives: one may recognize fellow members as merely "bad" like oneself and, therefore, unworthy. Or, alternatively, one might see them and oneself as like victims of the labeling and deprivations of an imperfect society and make common cause to change society's perceptions and practices.

This ideological variable is important among self-help groups and is somewhat akin to Edward Sagarin's distinction, which we have cited earlier. It would seem to have particular impact on ex-convict groups, since the degree of mutual trust that can emerge and the resulting strength and growth of the groups are directly affected.

Unlike other ex-prisoner groups, Seventh Step resembles the "anonymous" groups in having a quasi-religious formula for self-help. There are "Seven Steps," instead of A.A.'s fourteen, based, as in the latter, on the redemptive personal experience of a charismatic founder.

Because its members have been in prison, the social stigma they face is pervasive and extreme—not at all glamorous or easy to identify with. Perhaps for these reasons, the organization does not seem to have much ability to attract support from rich or influential people in the community. While some chapters work diligently on public education, the group as a whole lacks public relations resources and help from the media.

In efforts to improve the social position of ex-convicts, one might expect Seventh Step to seek support from and to influence policies of the courts, the police, probation and parole services, the legal profession, and so on. But its efforts in such directions seem sporadic, and thus far from being very effective. In some prisons, Seventh Step chapters do undertake predischarge counseling.

Like other small and weak organizations, Seventh Step has been riven by internal dissension and schisms—at least partly from the lack of mutual trust to which we have referred.

The Fortune Society
The most successful of the ex-prisoner groups in terms of its

speed of growth and public influence is the Fortune Society, which was spontaneously organized by members of the audience of an off-Broadway play, *Fortune and Men's Eyes*, dealing with the sufferings of men in prison.

In contrast to ex-prisoner groups, which accept the stigmatized position of their members, believe in personal redemption, and work chiefly on adaptive problems of members, the Fortune Society has a defined ideology of protest, takes a militant view of the need for radical prison and other social reforms. It has supported prison revolts, such as the one at Attica State Prison. It is deeply involved in criticism of the police, the judicial system, the legal profession, and in the way convicts and ex-convicts are socially stereotyped and scapegoated.

The following excerpts from an article by an English observer, Nancy Hodgkin, describe the Fortune Society's origin, outlook, and concerns.

Behind an enormous boarding above the Victoria Theatre on Broadway in Times Square, New York, is a small, crowded office. The walls are covered with playbills. There is a good bit of noise and a lot of coming and going. It is the office of David Rothenberg, a theater publicity director. He is a rather pale, worried-looking young man and he did the publicity for the play Fortune and Men's Eyes, *written by an ex-convict about life (and death) in prison, which was put on at an off-Broadway theater in 1967.*

Discussions began to take place on certain nights in the auditorium after the fall of the curtain. Ex-convicts in the audience found out that the rest of the audience had very little idea of what life in an American prison is like today. Disturbed at the lack of understanding shown, they then decided to do something about it—without much idea of what they could do. At this point, David Rothenberg came into the picture. If he had not done so, it is unlikely that any effective action would have been taken, ex-convicts not usually having the knowledge of publicity and organizing skills necessary to transform an idea into an enterprise. Further, they had neither money nor premises. David

Rothenberg provided the expertise, and his tiny office became their headquarters. Soon they managed to drum up a few voluntary contributions.

At first they had no very clear idea as to how their society—they called it the Fortune Society—should develop. They began to go out in small teams to speak to groups—civic groups, church groups, schools, colleges, and clubs. There was some initial opposition from heads of schools to the idea of their pupils hobnobbing with ex-convicts, but a gradually developing good public image—particularly when they began to be in demand on radio and television programs—changed this.

Now they have more requests than they can cope with. They have a weekly New York radio program every Sunday evening at 7:30 P.M., which is repeated on Monday morning, and they make guest appearances on other programs.

When they are speaking in public, the Fortune Society representatives regard themselves as ambassadors. I was impressed by the easy way they behaved in the extraordinarily elegant, almost baronial setting of Finch College. The Fortune Society was invited to the college by the girls themselves and no staff were at the meeting. When it came to queston time, the girls asked such questions as: What were the Fortune Society's relations with the parole and probation services? Was it easy to get drugs in prison? To the latter, the answer was, "Yes, through the guards."

At some point in every meeting David Rothenberg makes the point that nearly all members of the Fortune Society, including those present, had at one time been labeled incorrigible—"hardened criminals." "These men," he says, "are proof that change is possible."

One main obstacle in the way of justice, the Fortune Society says, is the practice of "plea bargaining," with its disregard for the guilt or innocence of the accused. This practice seems to be so taken for granted in the United States that lawyers are surprised at the Fortune Society's condemnation of it.[4]

Of interest is the Fortune Society's monthly newsletter. Its mailing list, which began with seven names in November 1967, now has more than fifteen thousand. Anyone who asks can be put on the list, and names are collected at the end of every speaking engagement. No charge is made for this newsletter, mainly because it is sent to prisons all over the United States, to any convict who wants it.

Among the difficulties that the Fortune Society often comes up against are the anomalies of the parole system. Parole varies from state to state to such an extent that not a single regulation appears in every one of the fifty states. One state includes a regulation that the parolee should refresh his memory by a periodic reread-ing of the parole document. As the parole period often extends over an extremely long period of time, these rules can be a considerable handicap to living as a free man and engaging in the normal life-style of a first-class citizen.

In Kansas, church attendance is compulsory for parolees. Also in Kansas, association or correspondence with "people of poor reputation"—specified generally as other ex-convicts or persons having a criminal or police record—is completely prohibited. Drinking liquor is prohibited in forty-one states, whereas the possession or sale of arms is only prohibited in twelve and permission has to be sought in fifteen; there is no restriction at all in twenty-one states. Permission to own or drive a motor vehicle must be obtained in thirty states and permission to marry in thirty-three. In eight states there is a curfew regulation. In thirty-eight states the man on parole must fill in a monthly report blank and send it to a central agency. In Iowa and Montana there is an absolute prohibition on crossing the state line but no inhibition in these two states on association with undesirables.

Several states ban association with undesirables, obviously a crucial issue for the Fortune Society. However, it is gradually overcoming this and gaining recognition by statutory bodies.

It is hard for prisoners to keep in touch with friends outside. The visiting records of a random sample of the inmate population of New Jersey State Prison over about a year showed that 41 percent had had no visitors at all.

A great deal has been written about the inmate social code in American jails, with its special terms and hierarchies. Surprisingly, most Fortune Society members seem to come from among the violent men, the "right guys," "real cons," rather than the "weak sisters," "merchants," or other less-well-thought-of characters. They were the ones who could take it and dish it out and maintain some modicum of self-respect under the worst conditions. Perhaps for this reason, they can respect and trust each other.

When men get out of jail, the society assumes an important role. In its own words:

Each week, 150 to 200 men and women released from prisons and jails come to the Fortune Society office. Our relationship, ex-convict to ex-convict, constitutes a major part of the Fortune Society's work.

Released inmates come to our office asking for a variety of things. Some are looking for jobs, some for housing, others for clothes or goods, many for help in fighting a drug or alcohol problem. Perhaps the greatest number of ex-inmates don't state why they come to our office . . . because they arrive out of their loneliness or a feeling that they don't belong anywhere in society. Often, men or women will stop by because someone with whom they did time is working here. For every man or woman who comes to the Fortune Society office, there is a different reason.

For all the importance and effort in finding a job, or a room, or some clothes, the single most important ingredient of a man-to-man, ex-con-to-ex-con relationship is the degree of understanding and identification that can be established.

The most difficult things that confront a man released from prison can be best understood and felt by another individual who has experienced the same feelings.

After years in an institution, the street poses a strange problem for the released inmate. Suddenly, he must make thousands of little decisions each day. While in prison, the state removed all decision-making from the man. We find many released inmates have difficulty at first in ordering food from a menu, deciding which bus or train to take, which street they should travel. The institutional life was the same, day after day, year after year, and in some cases, decade after decade.

Ex-convicts quickly recognize themselves in recently released inmates. They know the inner frustration, the vast sense of loneliness, the fear of failing, and the treacherous fact that prison has become "a security" rather than a deterrent for the lost parolee.

It is vitally essential for the released inmate, who feels that he is unique in this outcast role, to find out that others share the feeling. It is important for him to know that he can talk with someone when he is on the streets.

Many masks must be uncovered. Some parolees refuse to admit that the adjustment is a problem. Others resort immediately to old ways though they long for an alternative path.

All of this communication, ex-con to ex-con, cannot begin until the man is released from prison. Actually, it should begin while he is still an inmate, but most state officials negate meaningful communication for the inmates. As a result, the Fortune Society meets men after they are released.

We recognize all of the other aspects that a man must have to make it on the street, a job, a home, etc. We can only refer in those areas. That is not our expertise. We can make inquiry of employers about their hiring policy regarding ex-cons and check out hotels and apartment buildings which restrict former offenders. But we also know that many men with jobs have returned to prison—and that many parolees with a good apartment have been violated. We try to provide the foundation that makes all of the rest meaningful.

There is no formula. It takes concern, understanding, and love. The combination has to be there.[5]

Some experts on prisons believe that the utilization of ex-convicts is essential to this kind of successful contact with other ex-offenders. Milton Luger, director of New York State's Youth Division, thinks that some ex-offenders can do important, sensitive, skillful things that professional staffs cannot do.

This may be so, but a great deal of resistance would first have to be overcome. There are, for instance, forty states that have either statutory or administrative prohibitions against state agencies employing probationers or parolees. Not only regulations but also public opinion stand in the way of the wide employment of ex-offenders. A report issued recently by the Joint Commission for Correctional Manpower said that "a survey conducted for the commission found that the general public, while aware of the difficulties faced by the ex-offender in reentering the free community, is reluctant to have much contact with him and doubtful of his potential in anything but a menial job."

In this struggle, the Fortune Society may not have many material assets, but it has already succeeded in attaining a triumphant public image. Everywhere its members go, they seem to be welcomed and treated with respect. Their contact with schools is particularly valued, since they not only point out how false the glamorous picture of the criminal's life is, but also encourage boys and girls to take an active interest in what goes on in prisons, police stations, and other state institutions.

As Nancy Hodgkin concludes: "In the Fortune Society there is a truly common cause, among men of all races. It is, I think, something new. That these men, with their background of violence on both sides of the bars, have made common cause and come down on the side of reason is worth thinking about."[6]

Part III

What Makes
Self-Help
Groups Tick?

We find the true man only through group organization. The potentialities of the individual remain potentialities until they are released by group life. Man discovers his true nature, gains his true freedom only through the group.

—Mary P. Follett

To this point, we have presented case accounts and descriptions of the several main types of self-help groups. From our review of the available literature, it is regrettably clear that very little research has been conducted on the groups in general, or on particular aspects of structure, processes, or the relationships found in them.

The analysis and formulation of generalizations concerning such phenomena is part of our aim in this volume, and we introduce consideration of these topics by presenting two studies by social scientists in which self-help group processes and their effects on members are systematically analyzed. The two groups have very different foci; in our typology, the stutterers' organization would be classified as a "therapeutic" group, and the welfare mothers' group studied by Helene Levens is of the "social advocacy" type.

In Chapters 11 and 12, we draw upon these studies, other writings from the literature, and on our own observations and contacts with group members and ex-members in order to formulate generalizations about the structure, dynamics, and meaning to members of self-help and peer-support organizations.

9

Participation Patterns and Benefits of Membership in a Self-Help Organization of Stutterers

THOMASINA BORKMAN

Self-help organizations of stutterers had been thought to be nonexistent by students of social deviance and the stigmatized. Edwin Lemert, the one sociologist extensively interested in stutterers, wrote in 1970 that:

> *Stutterers—unlike the blind, the deaf, the physically handi-*
> *capped, narcotic addicts, criminals, and other deviants—do*
> *not form groups of their own, nor do they develop a subculture.*
> *Furthermore, they neither organize nor support therapy groups*
> *comparable to Alcoholics Anonymous.*[1]

Lemert's assertion must be revised to fit new evidence. Nineteen self-help organizations of stutterers are definitely known to have been initiated in the world, of which fourteen were in the United States.* Of the fourteen known associations in the United States, seven are currently functioning.

The oldest self-help group of stutterers in the United States that is still surviving was initiated in December 1965 for adults in a large metropolitan area on the East Coast. The study of this organization, which will be referred to as SO in this report, involved (1) eight months of participant observation and (2) a mail questionnaire survey of 190 stutterers known to have attended at least one SO meeting during this five-year period of its existence.

Frame of Reference and Research Questions

The discovery of a new species of self-help organization is exciting and raises a multiplicity of questions, especially from the perspective of the sociology of deviant behavior, voluntary associations, and social movements.

Two problem areas were explored in the study on which the present report is based. First, voluntary associations share a chronic problem of encouraging participation, reducing apathy, and increasing commitment to organizational goals and activities among their members. The major basis of differentiation of members is level of activity, not rank or status in the organization as it is in complex or formal organizations.[2] Level of participation is of special interest not only because of the general problems SO shares with other voluntary associations but also because of the

---

*This information was obtained during winter 1973 from personal correspondence and telephone communications directly with leaders from each of the organizations.

nature of stutterers and SO. Participation in SO is segmental with usually only one weekly meeting, the discouragement of outside friendships among SO members, and the encouragement of members to associate with nonstutterers. In addition, stutterers' problems of fear, shame, and nonfluency are more severe in secondary relationships, especially group activities, and probably impede the organizational participation of SO members.

The second problem area in this report is a major question of interest in self-help organizations of deviants and the stigmatized: What "therapy" is offered members and does it work? That is, to what extent do members reduce their deviant behavior, conform to society's norms, or learn to adjust to the stigmatization and lack of acceptance accorded them by society?

Before proceeding to describe the methods and findings of the study, a brief summary of the characteristics of the disorder of stuttering follows.

Characteristics of Stuttering | The degree of severity of stuttering is important because of its differential effects on social interaction. Severity refers to the number and intensity of blocks of speech, hesitations, repetitions, as well as to the length of time required to verbalize any bit of communication content. Mild stutterers have few and less noticeable disturbances of speech than moderate or severe stutterers. The time required for a mild stutterer to communicate any given amount of content may not be noticeably longer than for a fluent speaker. The speaking behavior of many mild stutterers would not even be defined as stuttering by the average layman. In contrast, the length of time and the speaking difficulties of the moderate and severe stutterer are apparent to everyone and their speaking behavior slows down and hinders the flow of conversation.

Adult stutterers attending the self-help organization (SO) are secondary deviants in Lemert's terms; that is, they play the role of stutterer, they have the self-concept of one, and most of them have nonfluent speech as well. The stuttering role includes fear of nonfluency in situations involving verbal participation. Lemert explains the process by which this develops:

When the stutterer is younger, he may enjoy free speech in cer-

tain situations; but as he grows older and nothing intervenes to alleviate his symptoms, the primacy of his stuttering role increases. There is a progressive involvement of his roles in many social situations. With each stuttering experience there are social failures and a corresponding sense of unpleasantness, inferiority, and anticipatory fears; the anticipatory fears create tensions and the greater likelihood of stuttering in each new situation he enters. Furthermore, the self-consciousness associated with normal learning errors and the tensions of extraneous social failures are likely to set off the stuttering response. The predominant self of which he is conscious at these times is that of a "stutterer," and more and more his social failures are subjectively taken as validation of the role.[3]

The etiology of stuttering is unknown, although there have been almost as many theories of the causation of stuttering as there are speech therapists studying the phenomenon. Likewise, there are a multitude of treatment methods, none of which consistently results in a cure of total fluency. Stutterers can become temporarily fluent by being distracted from their speaking behavior and their self. It appears as if many therapeutic methods are temporarily successful in increasing fluency because of this distraction principle. However, many sad tales are told by the graduates of these methods; six months or a year later, the pretherapy level of stuttering is often resumed.

The consequences of nonfluent speech for the stutterer have not been systematically counted and mapped in full detail. Underachievement in school, underemployment because of discrimination by employers who want fluent employees, and restricted social participation have been reported. Lemert argued that much of the restricted social participation is self-imposed by the stutterer rather than imposed on him by the social system.[4]

The societal reaction to stuttering is significantly different from the stutterer's reaction to his disorder. The contemporary middle-class American reaction to stuttering is that it is a minor form of deviation, which is mildly stigmatized.[5] Stuttering is not defined as a social problem or considered to be dysfunctional to society as is crime or mental illness. Unlike handicaps such as blindness, society accords little sympathy or attention to stuttering. Because it is regarded as a minor deviation, society regards it with indifference and unconcern.

In contrast, many adult stutterers regard the disorder as a serious problem in their life. Stigma interferes with normal interaction. In the case of the stutterer, the listener reaction is embarrassment, discomfort, laughter, or ridicule. Nonfluent speech spoils the identity of the speaker as a normal person and thus disqualifies him from full social acceptance.[6]

Methods of the Study

Participant observation of regular weekly meetings as well as intensive interviews with eight past and present leaders were conducted to obtain data (1) for a case study of the organization and (2) as inputs to the design of a mail questionnaire survey. Also, written materials produced by the organization, which were surprisingly numerous, were analyzed, including newsletters, annual reports from presidents, constitution and by-laws, and even a critical evaluation of the strengths and weaknesses of leadership methods of past presidents.

Study respondents were defined as adult stutterers known to have attended at least one meeting of SO between 1966 and April 1971 who were available to become members of the organization. Out-of-town visitors or nonresidents of the metropolitan area were excluded because they were not eligible to become active participants.

The 110 respondents completing questionnaires were predominantly young (44 percent were 25–34 years old and 68 percent were under 35 years of age), white (76 percent), males (77 percent), with very high educational levels (79 percent had attended college; 27 percent had advanced degrees), and the majority (54 percent) were married. In keeping with the high educational level was the skewed occupational distribution. Only 5 percent were in blue-collar occupations, 19 percent were in clerical-sales positions, and 47 percent were in professional or managerial occupations. The remaining 29 percent were students, housewives, or retired.

This highly educated group in high-prestige occupations presents a picture contrary to that usually portrayed as the fate of stutterers. The high socioeconomic level of SO is not characteristic of all self-help organizations. For example, Lofland and Lejeune found a range from low to high socioeconomic level in the Alcoholics Anonymous groups in New York City that they investigated.[7] The group appears to resemble joiners of voluntary associations in terms of background characteristics.[8] Unfortunately, there are no studies of the background characteristics of representative samples of adult stutterers with which to make a comparison with study respondents.

The only reasonable conclusion is that the study respondents are a highly self-selected group (in unknown ways) and do not resemble the universe of adult stutterers in terms of background characteristics. Conclusions from this study cannot be generalized to the universe of adult stutterers.

Summary of Findings and Conclusion

Organizational Analysis: Goals and Treatment of Stuttering | SO is a legally incorporated nonprofit voluntary association of and for stutterers. Membership is open to stutterers and anyone concerned with the problem. The organization was initiated and is controlled by stutterers. Professional speech therapists are welcome to participate in the organization but they are regarded as equals not as superiors in their knowledge of stuttering. Any efforts by professional speech therapists to control the organization or direct its activities would be quickly discouraged.

The major self-help goals of the organization are to help stutterers help themselves by (1) increasing their knowledge of stuttering and its treatment and (2) changing their attitudes toward their stuttering behavior, their self-concept, and the stigma they experience in social interaction. Increasing fluency of members is not a goal of SO, although it is hoped that increased fluency will be a by-product of achieving the other goals.

Organizational activities oriented toward achieving these goals for the membership include weekly group meetings in which stutterers can *talk* about their experiences and problems in an accepting, supportive atmosphere of fellow stutterers. Special speaking projects like lectures to community groups or TV presentations are periodically available. Lectures by speech therapists, psychologists, hypnotists, and others knowledgeable about stuttering are also given at weekly group meetings to increase members' information about stuttering and various treatment methods. Participating in these activities constitutes the "therapy" offered members.

SO ideology regarding the characteristics of stuttering, associated treatment techniques considered to be effective in ameliorating stuttering, the "therapy" offered members by the organization, and its organizational goals include increases in information about stuttering and the modification of negative attitudes of shame, fear of nonfluency, unwillingness to talk about stuttering, and lack of self-understanding. Increased fluency per se was not a goal of the organization.

Participation of Members | Unlike Alcoholics Anonymous or Synanon, participation in SO is limited and segmental. Active participants in the organization did not attend weekly meetings regularly but continued their involvement over two or more years and engaged in special speaking projects offered by the organization.

Few persons attended many meetings during one year only or attended frequently without getting involved in the special projects of the organization. It appears as if there are few members who maintain a minimal involvement with SO for any length of time. However, active participation in SO does not mean regular attendance at the fifty weekly meetings each year. These survey findings are consistent with the patterns of attendance observed at meetings and with a separate analysis made of attendees during the six-month participant observation period. Members do not come regularly to weekly meetings but maintain their membership and an active involvement over a period of several years. It was not uncommon to observe old members reappear after six months' absence or to see active members attend one meeting in a one- to two-month period. Of the stutterers attending during the six-month period between November 1970 and April 1971 for which attendance records were consistently kept, only 25 percent came to half or more of the meetings and 50 percent came to less than one-fourth of the meetings.

There was no association between SO participation and that in other voluntary associations. Striking differences were found, however, in SO participation and informal social participation. "Tasters" had very high levels of informal participation, with 58 percent indicating that they got together with friends, relatives, or co-workers three times a week or more. This group appears to have been too busy to have much time for SO. Dropouts were the least active in informal networks, with only 22 percent going out as often as three times a week and 51 percent who went out "a few times a month" or less. Medium and highly active participants were in between the other groups in frequency of informal social participation.

Joining and participating in a self-help association should be highly affected by self-defined need for the organization, from our general knowledge of voluntary associations. In turn, need should be partially determined by how serious the individual's problem is defined. Three items measured respondents' problems with stuttering: (1) extent of fear of nonfluency, (2) degree of stuttering, and (3) seriousness of stuttering as a problem in their life. These reflect major components of the severity of the stuttering problem as self-defined by the individual. The expectation was that for the inactive groups, the more serious the self-defined problem, the greater the need for help and, accordingly, the greater the willingness to participate in the organization.

A curvilinear relationship between severity of self-defined problem and activity level was found. The tasters and the highly active felt that their problems were mild in terms of all three indicators. Dropouts and medium active saw their problems as moderate-severe with the dropouts indicating the most severe problems.

The difference between tasters and dropouts is striking and supports the expectation that the more serious the problem, the more likely to participate. Tasters were mild stutterers with little fear of nonfluency and did not return to the organization after one visit. In contrast, dropouts who did return for more than one visit felt that they had severe problems with their stuttering and had a great need for the organization, but they dropped out after attending a few meetings. These findings suggest that SO fails to maintain the participation of some stutterers with severe problems, the ones with a definite need for the organization.

"Therapeutic" Effects | Of the respondents who had attended more than one meeting 65 to 75 percent reported that they gained some knowledge and had less negative attitudes toward their stuttering and themselves as a result of their organizational participation. The organization was most effective in modifying attitudes and in increasing information, which was consonant with their self-help goals. Attitudes toward stuttering and its treatment and the degree of stuttering were not associated with the amount or type of benefits received by members. The greater the participation in the organization, the more was gained cognitively, attitudinally, and behaviorally.

The complex theory of stuttering and its treatment espoused by the organization is at odds with the beliefs of many stutterers and professionals in speech therapy. No magic cure is promised, or even worse, no complete cure at all is thought to be possible. The treatment advocated is arduous, of long duration, and disapproving of easy solutions such as using mechanical devices or avoidance techniques. Stutterers looking for an instant cure through easily applied techniques would find the organizational theory incompatible with their expectations. Undecided stutterers with less definite beliefs would be more open to consider the theory but certainly not all would accept such a long, difficult road leading only to a minimal solution (becoming a comfortable stutterer).

The two inactive groups appear to be from different populations of stutterers. Tasters who only attended one meeting defined their stuttering problem as minor and were very active in a network of informal social participation, while the second group dropped out because their problems were most severe. Some severe stutterers undoubtedly left when they realized their hope for an instant cure could not be realized by participation in SO. Several inactives commented in their questionnaire that they left because no formal speech therapy was available. Perhaps the very severity of their speaking problems prevented some from accepting a therapy based on talking.

SO is somewhat effective in achieving self-help goals for its membership according to the subjective reports of members, but to gain much from the organization in ameliorating one's stuttering problem, a long-term active participation over two, three, or more years appears necessary. Little is gained by those attending a few times during one year only. SO is certainly not an instant self-help group.

In addition, a small percent (up to 7 percent) of attendees reported negative benefits of less fluency, more fear of nonfluency, and more shame of their stuttering after participating in the organization. The finding that dropouts had the most serious stuttering problems indicates that the organization may fail to help those most in need of its "therapy"; the organizational "therapy" may be effective only with stutterers with moderate-mild problems.

Additional research is of course needed to objectively ascertain the effectiveness of SO as a self-help organization, especially longitudinal studies in which members are followed over time to determine the extent to which the organization contributes to changes in their behavior, attitudes toward their stuttering, and their self-concept. Comparative studies of self-help organizations of stutterers would increase our understanding of organizational structures that facilitate or impede increased fluency, a more positive self-concept, and less negative attitudes toward stuttering.*

*The author is currently engaged in a comparative organizational analysis of the fourteen associations in the United States, and those in Sweden, Holland, and New Zealand with the support of a grant from the National Institute of Mental Health.

10

Organizational Affiliation and Powerlessness: A Case Study of the Welfare Poor

HELENE LEVENS

Now that middle-class America has rediscovered the poor there has been a plethora of studies designed to describe the life-style of those who are euphemistically termed "disadvantaged," "deprived," or "economically underprivileged." In their analyses of the social psychological attributes of those living in poverty, many social scientists have recurrently referred to pervasive feelings of powerlessness among the poor. . . . The poor are alternatively described as politically inactive and unorganized, fatalistic in their outlook on life, and generally lacking the conviction that it is within their power to affect their situation.

It has long been the belief of those who are concerned with problems of poverty that these feelings of powerlessness can be overcome by actively and meaningfully involving the poor in self-help community organizations. Through this kind of participation it is maintained that the poor will gain a sense that they can affect the world around them and that they can, through solidarity with others, organize successfully to alter their environment. Warren Haggstrom has suggested that participation in powerful neighborhood conflict organizations by the poor enhances their conception of their own worth and helps to overcome their feelings of powerlessness. Organization of the poor is seen by Warner Bloomberg as an effective strategy in combating feelings of dependency. Thus, in the view of many authors the sense of fatalism and the lack of destiny control prevalent among the poor can be ameliorated through their participation in self-help community action organizations.

Implicit in the analyses of these poverty experts are two untested propositions: (1) that there is a negative relationship between organizational affiliation and feelings of powerlessness such that those involved in a community organization of the poor would be less likely to feel powerless over their destinies than would non-affiliates and (2) that participation in community organizations *produces* feelings of destiny control. This paper is an attempt to test empirically the merits of the first proposition as well as to speculate upon the validity of the second.

A unique opportunity to test the relationship between organizational affiliation and powerlessness among the poor presented

SOURCE: Excerpted with permission from "Organizational Affiliation and Powerlessness: A Case Study of the Welfare Poor," *Social Problems,* vol. 16, no.1 (Summer 1968).

itself to the author during the summer of 1966. At that time welfare recipients throughout the nation—in particular, those women receiving Aid to Families with Dependent Children—were beginning to organize themselves into militant welfare recipients leagues designed to educate those receiving public assistance as to their legal entitlements and to press actively for the realization of these entitlements. . . .

One of these local league chapters provided a "natural" social laboratory in which the relationship between affiliation and powerlessness among the poor could be studied.

It was hypothesized that members of the Welfare Recipients League would have fewer feelings of powerlessness than nonmembers. For purposes of this study powerlessness was viewed as a social psychological construct manifesting itself in specific attitudes and behavior patterns thought to be characteristic of those living in poverty. The specific hypotheses to be treated in this study are:

1|Members of the Welfare Recipients League (WRL) are less likely than nonmembers to have a fatalistic outlook toward life.

2|Members of the WRL are more likely than nonmembers to perceive themselves as capable of exerting control over the problems that impinge upon them in their local environment.

3|Members of the WRL are more likely than nonmembers to engage in political activities designed to alter their life circumstances.

Several control variables possibly related to powerlessness were selected for use in the study:

Age|One of the accompaniments of the aging process is the feeling of rejection and social isolation. As people become older, they begin to see themselves as powerless to effect changes; this is especially true of the aging poor. They feel, and are, in fact, left behind, discarded, and rejected. Thus, associated with the aging process may be feelings of powerlessness and dependency.

Education|It is reasonable to assume that education and powerlessness are inversely related. Increasing one's educational training produces feelings of greater mastery over the environment. Knowledge is, after all, a source of power.

Work History | Empirical evidence suggests that there is a positive relationship between unemployment and powerlessness:

> *Prolonged unemployment typically leads to a deterioration of personality: passivity, apathy, anomia, listlessness, dissociation, lack of interest and of caring.* [1]

Welfare recipients who have had more "active" work histories, that is, those women who have been employed, are more likely than those who have never worked to feel that they can alter their life circumstances.

Length of Time on Aid to Families with Dependent Children (AFDC) | Women who have been receiving welfare for a long period of time are likely to become resigned to their dependent status and to perceive no egress from their present situation.

Number of Children | Confinement to the mother role probably results in feelings of powerlessness for the welfare mother; she may wish to improve her situation by seeking employment and involvement in the wider community but in most cases she is prevented from doing this because she cannot afford to hire a baby-sitter. Being a welfare mother with one or two children means that one's movement in the world—physically, socially, psychologically—is circumscribed. When one adds the presence of many children, it is a world with tight steel bands around it.

Number of Organizational Affiliations | Sociological literature is replete with studies demonstrating an inverse relationship between organizational affiliation and powerlessness. Differences in powerlessness between league members and nonmembers could conceivably be due to membership in other organizations.

Methods
The study sample of 131 AFDC mothers was comprised of 123 Negroes and 8 English-speaking Puerto Ricans living in a twelve-square-block slum community in a large northeastern city. Two types of respondents were needed: those who belonged to the

Welfare Recipients League and those who lived in the area served by the league but were not affiliated with it. From the outset, it became impossible to obtain a random sample of the community and league populations. The local welfare board refused to supply a list of AFDC recipients residing in the study area and the Welfare Recipients League, having only been in existence for six months, had no membership list available. The research population was limited to English-speaking Puerto Rican mothers. It should be noted that this limitation of the study population decreased the representative nature of the sample since neighborhood leaders familiar with the ethnic composition of the target area estimated that Puerto Ricans comprised approximately 40 percent of the population. Another problem presented by the block sampling method was the lack of welfare recipients in some of the dwelling units because of vacant apartments or the absence of AFDC welfare recipients in the dwelling unit assigned. In an effort to alleviate these problems, it was decided that each interviewer should go to every house on her assigned square block until such time as the quota for the block was reached. Every one of the twelve square blocks served by the Welfare Recipients League was sampled in this manner. Approximately 40 percent of the interviews were conducted on weekends and at night so as to increase the representative nature of the sample.

There were also methodological problems connected with obtaining a representative sample of league members. Since no membership list was available, several meetings of the Welfare Recipients League were attended by the researcher and at two of these meetings everyone present volunteered to be interviewed. Because of the practical difficulties encountered, the resulting sample is not a purely random one, and caution should be exercised in generalizing the findings.

The three interviewers employed in the study were themselves Negro AFDC mothers living in the target area. . . . The similarity of the interviewers' status and problems with those of the respondents helped them to establish immediate rapport with the subjects and served to increase the validity of the responses elicited. . . . The refusal rate was low, well below 5 percent. The interviewers' ability to empathize with the respondents encouraged the subjects to express themselves freely and openly. . . . In fact, interviewers often remarked on how eager the respondents were to share their personal problems, concerns, and opinions in the interview situation. The interviewers assured the researcher that this kind of reaction from the respondents would never have been elicited by white, middle-class interviewers. The use of indigenous personnel was a decided asset to the study.

The research instruments attempted to measure three different dimensions of powerlessness: fatalism, sense of control, and lack of political activism. A fatalistic orientation toward life—the belief that one's destiny is controlled by external and threatening forces over which one has no personal influence—was measured by means of eight attitude items patterned after those developed in a previous study.[2] After hearing each one of the following eight expressions read by the interviewer, the respondent was asked whether she strongly disagreed, disagreed, agreed, or strongly agreed with the item:

1 | My existence is completely under the control of destiny.

2 | The success I'm going to have was already in the cards when I was born, so I might as well accept it and not fight it.

3 | I have complete trust in destiny, which keeps me from worrying.

4 | There's no sense in taking a chance failing at something new, when I'm doing all right as I am.

5 | Fate determines what happens to me.

6 | I feel that nothing, or almost nothing, can change the opinion I currently hold of myself.

7 | Every human problem can be solved and every desire satisfied if destiny so wills.

8 | Let us eat, drink, and be merry, for tomorrow we die.

Arbitrary weights were attached to each of these forced choice responses and a total score for each respondent was computed. A follow-up item analysis resulted in the selection of five of the original eight (1,2,3,5,7) items which showed the greatest discrimination between high scorers and low scorers.

. . . Concepts of fate and destiny were not clearly understood by many respondents. In cases like these, interviewers were given specific instructions as to how to redefine the terms in a more lucid and meaningful manner. . . . A sizable proportion of respondents tended to concretize the meanings of the expressions in terms of their daily life experience and often responded to the statements in a very literal way.

An indication of general respondent difficulty and frustration in interpreting the attitude items can be seen in the following remarks:

"Lord have mercy! Where'd you get these questions from?"

"Is this part of the interview almost over?"

"Why in the world are you asking me these silly questions for?"

"What's this got to do with being on welfare?"

The extent to which the five measures which comprised the final fatalism scale lack validity is impossible to ascertain, for the interviewers did not systematically note the reaction of the respondents to the items. However, the apparent difficulty experienced by some subjects in interpreting the meaning of the items raises serious doubts about the basic validity that these indices have for members of a welfare population. It grows obvious that meaningful and valid measures of powerlessness may not as yet have been developed for the very population that is perennially being characterized as expressing the greatest degree of fatalism.

In an effort to measure powerlessness in a way that would be perceived as meaningful and concrete to women on welfare, a series of questions was developed to indicate whether the respondent defined herself as one who was able to control or influence problems that impinged upon her in her local environment. This perception of personal control over problems of immediate importance was termed as a "sense of control." . . .

Specifically, all respondents were asked the following series of questions:

1 | What are two or three things that you would like to see changed around here?

2 | Who do you think should change these things?

3 | Do you think there is anything YOU could do to change these things?

An affirmative reply to the third question was considered an indication of "high" sense of control.

The final dimension of powerlessness—lack of political activism—was measured by eliciting the number, date, and type of political rallies and demonstrations attended by the respondents within the year preceding the time of the interview. The nature of the political activities engaged in and the time during which participations occurred were particularly important to determine for, since its inception six months preceding the study, the league had actively supported, and in one instance initiated, many such events in the community. . . . Consequently, differential rates of participation in these political events between affiliates and non-affiliates could serve as an indicator of the extent to which the Welfare Recipients League effects behavioral changes in the political activism of its members. A person rated "high" on political activism was defined as one who had attended a political rally or demonstration within the six-month period after the creation of the league.

Findings

The data support the general hypothesis that there is a negative relationship between organizational affiliation and powerlessness among the welfare poor. *On each of the three dependent variables members of the Welfare Recipients League felt more powerful than nonmembers.* Specifically, 35 percent of the members had a fatalistic outlook toward life, whereas this same orientation was shared by 59 percent of the nonmember population. A high sense of control over one's immediate problems was expressed by 57 percent of the members, whereas only 24 percent of the nonaffiliates experienced a similar feeling of mastery. The most striking difference between the two populations occurred in the sphere of political activism: 78 percent of the members had participated in demonstrations and rallies within the six-month period after the establishment of the league, in contrast to 13 percent of the nonmembers.

How can these differences in powerlessness be explained? According to the poverty experts, the differences in powerlessness between members and nonmembers are directly attributable to the effects of organizational membership in the league per se. Advocates of the "selection theory" would maintain that those AFDC mothers who joined the league had few feelings of powerlessness even before joining the association. As has been previously indicated, the answer to the causal questions requires the utilization of an experimental and longitudinal research design. Since a study of this nature was not feasible, six control variables were utilized in the comparison of the member and nonmember populations. If a selective process were at work, we would expect that there would be significant differences between members and nonmembers on most of the variables.

No significant differences between members and nonmembers are found on four of the six control variables. Specifically, members and nonmembers do not differ with respect to age, education, number of children, and number of organizational affiliations. The fact that the groups do not differ on certain demographic variables would seem to suggest that differential selection was not primarily responsible for differences in feelings of powerlessness. Further, indirect evidence of the fact that the league does not selectively recruit more powerful recipients is to be seen in members' response to the question, "Why did you join the league?" The overwhelming majority (72 percent) replied, "To get help from the league with my problems." This type of response suggests that most women who join the league feel initially incapable of solving their own problems, that is, they feel powerless.

Members do differ from nonmembers with respect to employment history and length of time on AFDC. The league members are more likely to have held one or more jobs between 1963 and 1966 and to have been on welfare less than three years. Why should active work histories and short-term welfare support be more characteristic attributes of members? Perhaps women who have held jobs and who have managed—if only briefly—to break the cycle of dependency, become more determined to improve their life situations, and perceive organizations like the league as a means toward this end, whereas women who have remained unemployed—who have not been thrown into abrasive contact with the "outside" world—are more likely to accept the status quo. Perhaps, also, the cumulative effects of being on welfare for a prolonged period of time produce feelings of such crippling despair and resignation that the welfare mother no longer believes that there is anything she can do to better her condition; the appeals for militant action issued by welfare client organizations like the league may go unheeded by women such as these. Witness the following member's remark:

> *The Welfare Department ties too many people down around here. You stay on Welfare the way it's set up now and you can't make progress even when you try. So after a while on welfare a lot of people just give up tryin'. They just don't care anymore.*

Women newly added to welfare rolls may not have had time to adopt the defeatist attitudes associated with their recently acquired dependent status. These women may be more receptive to external influences like the league.

In an effort to eliminate the possible "contaminating" effects of work history and the length of time on AFDC, these two variables were held constant in examining the relationship of league membership to powerlessness. If league membership is a key explanatory variable in accounting for differences in powerlessness between the two groups, then there should continue to be a difference between affiliates and nonaffiliates even when the effects of work history and the length of time on welfare are controlled.

When the effects of work history and the length of time on AFDC are held constant, a far greater percentage of nonmembers than members remains high on fatalism, low on sense of control, and low on political activism. On almost all of the comparisons, the difference in powerlessness between members and nonmembers is as great or greater when work history and the length of time on AFDC are controlled as when they are not. Apparently the difference in powerlessness between members and nonmembers cannot be explained by these two variables.

Each measure of powerlessness can be considered separately. When controlling for work history and the length of time on AFDC, nonaffiliates continue to be less likely than affiliates to participate in political rallies and demonstrations. . . .

It would appear that the league, through the socialization of its members, was instrumental in effecting changes in political participation. The data suggest that, once having joined the league, members were exposed to social pressure from others within the organization to participate in community rallies and demonstrations. Evidence of this social pressure is seen in the following members' remarks, which are in no way atypical:

Of course I goes to rallies. I believe in them now. And besides— the others would kill me if I didn't show up!

I demonstrated 'cause I thought we all had to back each other up so's we could make ourselves heard. . . . And I also went because if I didn't I would have never heard the end of it! The girls would have been talking about me like a dog!

Participation in political rallies and demonstrations would appear to be an outgrowth of league membership, for attendance at such events was considered an integral part of the membership role. In the process of fulfilling these role expectations, members began to feel as though they could do somethimg to improve the community in which they lived. . . .

. . . A low sense of control over one's immediate problems was expressed by 43 percent of the members and 77 percent of the nonmembers in the uncontrolled population. After controlling for long-term AFDC and active work history, the relationship between lack of affiliation and low sense of control remains identical or is even higher than it was before. When the effects of short-term AFDC and inactive work history are not allowed to operate, the relationship between lack of affiliation and low sense of control decreased only slightly.

A fatalistic view toward life was shared by 35 percent of the members in sharp contrast to 59 percent of the nonmembers in the uncontrolled sample. After controlling for short-term AFDC and active work history, differences between members and nonmembers in fatalism became even more distinctive. In contrast, differences in attitudes of fatalism are reduced when long-term AFDC and inactive work history are held constant.

The fact that differences in feelings of personal control and fatalism are not as distinctive when controlling on certain variables should not be taken to mean that organizational affiliation plays no part in effecting attitudinal changes among members. Rather than viewing the selection and socialization theories as separate explanatory schemes, it might perhaps be more useful to explain affiliates' greater feelings of efficacy as a product of selection in combination with the experience of organizational participation. Such an explanation, however, is only one in a series of possible interpretations that might be offered to account for the results of the present study. Other viable explanations should seriously be considered.

Powerlessness is a multifaceted construct, manifesting itself in diverse ways. Further, the sense of powerlessness can occur in many contexts, ranging from powerlessness with respect to the intimate spheres of friendship and affection, to powerlessness in the domains of work and international affairs. Perhaps affiliation in a welfare client organization decreases recipients' feelings of powerlessness most dramatically in connection with the welfare situation itself. Thus, if powerlessness had been operationally defined as the welfare recipient's perceived inability to make demands upon her caseworker, the effects of organizational affiliation might have been in even greater evidence. When asked what joining the league had meant to her, one respondent replied emphatically:

> Now that I know more about the welfare and know what I can or can't have I demand my rights and get more respect from my investigator. He can't treat me like I was dirt no more.

The fact that this study was conducted only six months after the Welfare Recipients League had been established in the community might have influenced the results obtained. It is conceivable that the impact of league membership on attitudes of powerlessness would have been more forcefully demonstrated at some later point in the league's development. The impact of organizational affiliation at a given point in time may not be uniform on its members; some women may be responsive to league influence after attending one or two meetings, whereas others may be affected by the organization only after they have been in attendance for many months. It could be, for example, that chronic welfare dependents—women who have been on long-term AFDC and without work—require extensive exposure to the league and its activities in order to overcome the feelings of fatalism which have been a part of their lives for so long. Thus, the differential response of league members to affiliation may be a function of the arbitrary and premature timing of the study. . . .

Summary

The results supported the hypothesis that there was a negative relationship between powerlessness and membership in the welfare client organization. Further analysis revealed that there were no differences between the two groups with respect to age, education, number of children, and number of other organizational memberships, suggesting that differential selection on these characteristics was not primarily responsible for differences in powerlessness. Members were more likely than nonmembers to have had active work histories and short-term welfare support. After these two variables were controlled, the relationship between powerlessness and affiliation was as great or greater than it had been before. It would appear that the impact of the league was greatest in effecting changes in political activism. Attitudes of powerlessness, although not changed dramatically for all segments of the affiliated population, were sizably reduced by membership in the league. Affiliation in a welfare client organization appears to be a powerful weapon with which to combat powerlessness among the welfare poor. In the words of the league president:

The people that come to the league been down for so long they don't know how to get up. They says, "Can I actually hold a conversation with someone else out in the street? Can I actually demand things from my investigator?" And that's why I think the Welfare League has done more for the people in this neighborhood than anything before it. More and more mothers are doing volunteer work for us. After a while with the league they get to see that there's a lot of things they can do to help theirselves. And then they're on their way.

11

Intra-Group Dynamics in Self-Help Organizations

Introduction

We have, thus far, examined contemporary self-help groups from several angles of vision: their origin and history, their significance as social movements, their goals and directions, their relationship to the mainstream and some tributaries of American social life. We have also attempted to classify them by some functional criteria. In the accounts of different categories of groups presented to the reader for illustrative purposes, certain observable features have recurred—the groups' patterns of origin, growth, and development; their saliency for members; their internal organization; their connectedness to the wider world.

In this chapter we examine dynamic factors and social processes within these groups and delineate the forces, both internal and external, that produce these recurrent phenomena. We review self-help organizational dynamics while considering certain key questions: What is it that holds self-help groups together? What kinds of membership interaction occur? What benefits do members derive? Or, more specifically:

Why do people choose to join self-help groups?

What expectations do joiners have?

Are these different for self-help groups than for other types of organizations?

What satisfactions does the new member find in the self-help group?

What gains does membership in the group afford?

Do these continue?

What is the nature of member participation? Is it similar to or different from that in other types of organizations?

Reasons for Joining

Broadly speaking, people join self-help groups for two reasons. First, as we have noted, many persons are frustrated and rejected by the larger society and its institutions, have feelings of powerlessness over decisions that affect their lives, experience a helpless inability to change a "world they never made." Second, the individual in this bureaucratic age is classified, categorized, numbered, ranked, and labeled; he feels manipulated, spindled—forgotten. Many persons—perhaps a majority—find that the society which glorifies and claims to nurture individuality and freedom has at the same time depersonalized them into lockstep conformity.

Particularly in times like the present, when we are experiencing rapid changes in social values, many find intolerable the strains, incongruities, and incompatibilities in the statuses and social roles into which they have been born and grew up. They cannot unquestionably accept the old identities, social positions, or attitudes; they seek acceptable new ones. Often they grasp at opportunities for face-to-face interactions with peers, with others holding similar values and desires. They initiate friendships, join social clubs, register with a political party, participate in organized communal activities, attend professional meetings. When these efforts do not provide enough personal gratification they may originate *new groups,* seeking in them affiliations and interactions that are more satisfying, and which provide that commonality and support that is a basic human need.

Many self-help or mutual aid groups attract individuals who are considered by society and have come to consider themselves as rejects, nonconformists, deviants. Society at large and their personal history have cast them into roles they do not relish—the alcoholic, the ex-mental patient, the compulsive gambler, the ex-convict, and so on. By encountering social disapproval, many such people are *pushed* into seeking out substitute group relationships. Ensuing rebuffs become internalized into a sense of failure and stigma frequently reinforced by unsatisfactory personal relationships in their families and elsewhere. Feeling victimized and alone, they are *pulled* by personal need into joining a self-help activity, especially if there is an appropriate organization, both visible and accessible, which seems to offer the promise of personal acceptance and satisfactions.

Here, however, we encounter a feature peculiar to the self-help group—the prospective member often must define himself as in need of the help of others. A "problem" gambler who seeks acceptance into Gamblers Anonymous must affirm, not deny, his problem. In joining he makes a contract with the group: they will confront together the fact they he is a compulsive gambler. He must want help from others strongly enough to *risk* the pain, embarrassment, or guilt of such self-exposure. The precondition for entry into many other groups is similar.

The Factors of Self-Selection and Emulation

A high degree of self-selection and self-definition is thus found in the composition of the membership of self-help groups. Addicts entering Synanon are often *in extremis* when they first knock on the door, yet these desperate folk agree to go "cold turkey" and endure the physiological horrors of withdrawal in order to remain. The "successful" joiner who sticks it out may experience pain, self-consciousness, and, at the very least, ambivalence; concurrently he is motivated by group support to make the effort. Devices such as "sponsors," the "buddy" system of A.A., or the mobilization of group pressures as in the Synanon Game are examples of how self-help groups enhance self-definition through different kinds of support systems.

Simple imitation is sometimes a contributing factor in attaching oneself to a group or in forming new ones. Edward Sagarin observes that

> *Any group's existence, let alone its publicity and alleged success, suggests to those in an analogous situation the possibilities and advantages accruing from the formation of similar organizations. Although people are prone to establish formal associations . . . they are more likely to do so when successful precedents have been set.* [1]

Many groups, of course, have emulated A.A.; to name a few, Gamblers Anonymous, Narcotics Anonymous, Overeaters Anonymous, Illegitimates Anonymous. These imitators usually take a similar name, and several have adapted the A.A. format—an opening prayer, a series of "steps" that must be acknowledged, the invoking of the Deity, and so forth. *Doing it yourself* now enjoys positive social sanction—the reactions to new self-help groups are generally favorable from the media and other opinion molders. The last few years have witnessed the rise of countless consumer self-help organizations, from shoppers' guides and food co-ops to honesty and truth consumer leagues in the Ralph Nader tradition.

Influences from Without

David Riesman has suggested that for most Americans, *external referees* are the most meaningful source of self-esteem and evaluation of one's effectiveness in coping with the exigencies of daily living. The reactions of important others are the primary data for self-evaluation. Riesman's "outer-directed" man has long since replaced the rugged American frontier individualist who found in his own conscience the sources of his self-esteem.

The findings of several social science investigations have also pointed out that human beings have a drive to maintain a sense of *consonance* or *harmony* of their opinions, attitudes, and beliefs. When a fundamental aspect of a person's life is "incongruent," he attempts to reduce the incongruence by reinterpreting observations about himself to fit the perceptions held by others; or he may seek to revise these perceptions by joining a self-help group. In this lies the self-help group's distinct role in identity (re)establishment.

The new member uses it as a *reference group,* that is, as a point of reference for his own perspectives. By affiliating, the member commences a journey, of which one of the goals is to reduce personal "dissonance" and the social stigma and anxiety previously experienced. Membership in the self-help group facilitates the taking of first steps toward changing self-perception and identity.

In such a quest, why join a *self-help* group in preference to some other kind? The answer is simple. Most informal social groups, especially those sanctioned by the dominant society, offer little *emotional* sustenance toward the resolution of personal problems, the establishment of identity, or the satisfaction of deep personal needs. Joining a social club, church group, political party, or trade union usually cannot bring about such changes or provide such direct personal help.

Resolving Personal Dilemmas

In addition to helping the newcomer perceive and deal with his *immediate social reality* more satisfactorily, self-help groups aid their members in finding workable approaches to many personal dilemmas by means of:[2]

1 | Developing and sustaining a coherent view of the world and the member's place in it.

2 | Helping the member learn new and more gratifying behavior.

3 | Helping the member tap his unconscious feelings.

4 | Fortifying the member's self-image and pride.

5 | Helping the member achieve more environmental mastery by uncovering or discovering his competence and by using the competence of each member to the fullest.

6 | Increasing the individual's coping abilities through his participation in group tasks of graduated difficulty.

7 | Advancing the member to new levels of self-perception and status within the group and when he feels ready to leave it.

Not all groups aid their members in each of these tasks. Nor do they necessarily follow a particular sequence. The group's ability to meet any individual's needs depends upon several factors: (1) its function and goals—whether social, educational, therapeutic, political, or mixed; (2) the degree of control exercised by the group's structure; (3) the recognition of the group by the larger community; and (4) the severity of the member's stigma or handicap.

To illustrate: (1) The rank and file of the Gay Liberation Movement, an assertive self-help type of group, will have a different view of what constitutes "environmental mastery" for them than the participants in a conforming or assimilative group like Parents Anonymous. (2) Synanon, with its tightly knit authoritarian structure, adheres to a view of the advancement of its "cured" members—who move into "the family" for perpetuity—that is not held by most other self-help groups. (3) Dead Numbers, a Canadian ex-convict group, feels itself successful if its former inmates, after a year or two on parole, *no longer want any connection with the group* and have merged into the mainstream society. Sponsored by the major Canadian agency for prison reform, Dead Numbers is chiefly concerned with its members' *behavioral adaptation* to regular jobs, stable personal and family life, and the nonuse of alcohol and drugs.

Levels of Participation and Communication

In self-help groups it is a tenet of philosophy and practice that leadership is determined from within. This accentuates what William Cameron has called the "we group" syndrome rather than the "us group" syndrome.[3] Contributing to the "we" feeling is a pervasive social atmosphere and sanction *that passivity is not acceptable.* Cohesiveness is fostered by the norm that group members are expected to conform to the standards of mutual helpfulness and cooperation. Status is conferred by personal involvement in furthering the interests of the group. Because of the intimacy of group size and interaction, members' capacity to contribute is readily assessed; peer pressures and group rituals become effective in controlling noncooperative behaviors. Take Off Pounds (TOPS) offers a dramatized procedure:

> . . . *At the beginning of the agenda, each member must be weighed by an official Weight Recorder. Weights are recorded on Weight Charts and losses or gains for the week are computed. Members weighing less than they did at the previous meeting are designated as "Tops," and are decorated with a cardboard heart specifying the amount of weight lost. Members whose weight has remained constant are labeled "Turtles." Members whose weight has increased become "Pigs" and have to wear a pig-shaped label or bib.*[4]

In addition to being evaluated for what they do, members of some self-help groups are pressured to have correct *attitudes* as well:

> *My name is Larry and I am an alcoholic. I have been an alcoholic for as long as I can remember. I guess I took my first drink when I was twelve, when I was playing with some older kids and they had some wine. I thought I'd be a wise guy, a big shot, and show them I could drink too. . . . So I started then, and it seems like I didn't stop for twenty years. . . . The first thing I learned in AA was that I was an alcoholic, and that an alcoholic can't control his liquor. He has to give it up. That was four years ago, and from the day I entered this room my life has changed completely.*[5]

This ritualistic confession made in front of an audience of peers is found in many groups. Whether stated individually as in A.A., G.A., or Narcotics Anonymous, or emanating from a group discussion as in the Synanon Game, such confessions are ritualized testimonials to the *wisdom of the group*. The wisdom is repeated and emphasized many times as reinforcement experiences that are shared by all.

More research is needed on the implications of such confessional happenings. One suspects, however, that a pledge made in public to abstain from drugs, alcohol, gambling—or to try to reduce one's feelings of self-pity—is a powerful lever of social control, soon becoming internalized.

The potential for change and the processes
by which it occurs in individuals and institutions are closely interrelated matters.
—Harris B. Peck, M.D.

12

Group Structures and Formats in Self-Help Organizations

What does the new member see
and hear when he begins to participate in a self-help group? First of
all he observes a gathering of persons usually totaling no more than

twenty. This seems to be a pattern self-help groups have evolved independently. Research in a variety of group settings has pretty firmly established that fifteen to twenty individuals constitute the upper limit for optimal communication, but the practice within self-help groups has probably not been affected by these studies.

Total membership of many self-help groups' sponsoring organizations is in many cases quite large—counted in the thousands and tens of thousands. As in other voluntary organizations having an international, national, or regional base, one finds the usual situation of local units or chapters. While some large national voluntary organizations undoubtedly do feature autonomy for their local units, practically all nationally and regionally headquartered self-help associations, operationally speaking, are structured for local autonomy. From the vantage point of self-help associations such a relationship is deemed essential for the emergence of organizational cohesion. And the leadership of self-help groups join with many contemporary critics of big institutions to emphasize the values of decentralization. "Doing it ourselves," either intuitively or functionally, is in keeping with most members' preferred wishes.

A second factor is the oft observed frequency of contact among new and veteran members. The sustained nature of this interaction promotes group cohesion of a high order and does so with surprising rapidity. There is still another factor setting off other voluntary groups from the self-help type: the extent to which decentralization leads to the emergence of the *small group as a structural and symbolic reality* for self-help associations and *small group behavior* as the most normative expression of membership interaction.

In very general terms a group can be conceived of as a plurality of individuals having something in common that makes a difference to them. However, the definition of a *small group* implies something more tangible and more delimiting. Thus Bernard Berelson and Gary Steiner define a small group as

> an aggregate of people . . . who associate together in face-to-face relations over an extended period of time, who differentiate themselves from others around them, who are mutually aware

*of their membership in the group and whose personal relations
are taken as an end in itself.*[1]

In other words it may prove useful to view self-help groups as
small groups—and borrowing a phrase from Clovis Shepard—
engaged in perpetuating "a network of affective relations."[2] Just
how effective can be gauged by noting how much the new member utilizes the structures set up for him and (eventually) by him
to (1) obtain help without the unequal status resulting from encounters with professionals, (2) move into a *shared* authority
system, (3) achieve self-validation, (4) obtain direct services
within the group, and (5) perceive his *own* social reality more
clearly in a relatively short time span.

Who's in Charge?
If the newcomer looks for a professional "helper"—social
worker, physician, psychologist, educator—as the group's prime
mover or catalyst, he will usually not find one. The climate, the
structure, the formal and informal patterning of social statuses
along with rules for participation *minimizes the playing of professional roles,* more often than not limiting professionals to an advi-
sory or consultative capacity, or to no more than coeval status.

The newcomer may initially conclude that the positions of authority correspond to his experience in other groups, with structured roles, such as president, vice-president, secretary,
treasurer. But he may also perceive something else. Officers of
self-help groups do not possess authority simply because of the
prestige they have in the outside world. The unspoken expectation is that each member carries a marshal's baton in his knap-
sack and at some point will contribute to leadership. The
authority and sanction of leadership is achieved or earned rather
than ascribed.

What Does the Self-Help Group Do for Its Members?
The self-help group first of all provides *concrete services;* it
helps the member determine what assistance he can most readily
receive and what would be most beneficial to him without his
being made to feel guilty or overwhelmed. Operation Bootstrap

teaches its people new social and technical skills, shows them they are not alone in a hostile white world, and provides employment for them. It offers baby-sitting and day-care services for mothers within the particular cultural framework of the black ghetto dweller. Parents without Partners helps its members become knowledgeable about the legalities of alimony and child support. TOPS (Take Off Pounds) provides a methodology and an atmosphere of cheerful competition in weight reducing.

Self-help groups continuously open themselves up for *inspection* and *assessment* by old-timers and potential recruits in terms of the concrete benefits that might accrue from membership. The groups also enable the new member to *perceive* his social reality more clearly or in a different way. Thus, Schizophrenics Anonymous denies that schizophrenia is psychogenic in origin, believing it to be a biochemical disorder (or group of disorders) that causes changes in *perception* and behavior. Stutterers Anonymous deals with and helps members overcome the feeling that they will be rejected because of their speech problems.

While the self-help groups usually do not promise members that they can be helped quickly, they do provide evidence of sincere concern. The message is: *You can count on us.* Paradoxically, the new member is told initially that he should rely upon his peers *more*, so that later on he will need to rely upon them *less*. . .

Group Structure as a Facilitator of Communication

It is reasonable to assume that a system has to evolve to promote effective communication within the group. On joining, a new member will have to be socialized into the group, learn how to perform his assigned roles.

The structures of Synanon and X-Kalay accomplish this through a division of labor. A new member is usually assigned a menial role. Specialization of activities is an accepted norm; regulation and *exchange* are needed among all residents, since each cannot do his thing or get his needs met simultaneously. The accepted division of labor is a vehicle for communicating such group values as respect for common property, the exchange of services through barter and bargaining, and the expectation of mutual emotional support.

Characteristically, self-help groups are marked by *equal status contacts*, despite hierarchical structures. The patterns of communication are from equal to equal rather than from subordinates to superiors. Status is achieved by example and leadership. X-Kalay's motto, "Character is the only rank," may be only an ideal, but suggests a direction. Status can be achieved by being a generous giver as well as a recipient of aid. Matthew Dumont, interestingly, discusses the distinction between the social authority structures in ex-addict self-help groups and that in traditional psychiatric wards with drug-dependent patients:

> In the self-help center there is little or no difference between the formal and the informal hierarchy. In a sense, there is only a formalized, informal hierarchy with decision-making openly and unashamedly a peer group phenomenon. Attitudes about one another are expressed freely so that everyone knows who is loved, who is hated, who is feared, and who is respected. . . . What seems to characterize the psychiatric ward is a kaleidoscopic array of diffuse authority structures, an inarticulate ecology of control mechanisms into which is thrust the patient, already burdened with the ambivalence about authority which characterizes drug dependence. . . .

> . . . The most important distinction between the authority structure of the self-help program and that of the psychiatric ward is that the former is open and the latter closed. No matter how oppressive or humiliating being at the bottom of the ladder in the self-help program is, there is always the possibility of reaching the top. In fact, achieving the top is the purpose of the program. . . . On a psychiatric ward, regardless of how well you behave, how much "health" you manifest . . . you can never attain the position of a nurse or a doctor. Authority, diffuse as it is, remains forever unattainable, and regardless of one's inherent or emergent capacities, the low status of patienthood remains an onus until the moment of discharge when the stigma of ex-patienthood may continue to exact its toll. [3]

One may view patterns of communication and participation as

taking place in the context of changing group climates or milieus. At different stages in its growth the self-help group acts both as a psyche group and a socio-group. According to Helen Hall Jennings, "psyche" groups are personal, spontaneous, and effective; tnat is, they have a primary group atmosphere; socio-groups are more formal and impersonal. "Operationally" speaking, the psyche group is defined in terms of the choices made by the group members . . . of those with whom they would like to *relax;* the socio-group is defined by choice of those with whom they would like to *work.*[4] We may posit communication as taking place then on an informal basis, for example, bull-sessions among the participants, or on more highly structured, formalized occasions, such as the confessional. In either case, however, communication patterns are set up as to allow mutual aid and psychic support to become manifest.

Katherine Whiteside Taylor finds Helen Jennings's distinction useful in her discussion of parent-child preschool cooperatives:

The best parent coops are both psyche and socio-groups. . . . Focused as they are on significant activities that demand continual joint study, planning and operating, they became sociogroups. Through evolving common insights and attitudes, sharing concerns, wishes, feelings, they often become very real psyche groups as well. Cooperatives may start as either one or the other, as a group of interested friends and neighbors who are already a psyche group, or as a group wanting to establish a nursery school for their children. The cohesiveness and effectiveness of socio-groups increases in direct proportion as they become a psyche group also.[5]

Leadership and Followership

Leadership has been defined as "the set of functions through which the group coordinates the efforts of individuals." All groups have one or more persons who act in that capacity; the degree to which they are successful depends upon how well such leaders satisfy individuals as well as reflect and meet the purposes of the group. As we indicated earlier, in self-help groups the power of the leader is the power the group delegates to him.

W. R. Bion's words appear to have particular relevance for authority figures in self-help groups; he views leadership "as the facilitation of group skill in diagnosing its own state of emotion."[6] But there are several levels of complexity contained in this statement, when referring to self-help groups. Firstly, the appropriate leader in an assertive group (Welfare Rights Committee) might find her leadership style out of phase with the membership in an assimilative group (Parents Without Partners). Leaders who function well in psyche group situations might not be effective in action considerations of the socio-group. Leadership qualities may be different when self-help groups reach a higher level of organizational development than when they are first formed. There is evidence that the group's first leaders are often those with charismatic qualities, *expressive* leaders who may eventually give way to more instrumental authority figures. Synanon, X-Kalay, Seventh Step, and A.A. have retained some of their original leaders through successive stages of growth, but in practically every case, the original leaders had been supplemented by others, who have focused upon *goal achievements* rather than upon *group maintenance*.

The norms of the group condition members' expectations of how leaders are expected to perform. Thus, Recovery meetings are conducted by group leaders who are known to be "nervous" themselves. Leaders are presumed to have the same kinds of problems as members and do not regard themselves as "cured."

The traditional dichotomy between leader and led, the authority figure and the follower without authority, tends to be reduced, if not altogether eliminated, in mutual aid groups. By definition, self-help groups emphasize *reciprocal* assistance. No leader can be put in a position whereby he alone administers material or psychic assistance to others but *claims* none need be administered to him. Of course, if the leader feels that he no longer requires a role to play in the organization, he may step down.

Stress and Strain within the Self-Help Group

When a group flounders and declines, its purposes may have been achieved or may have ceased to be important to members. Or it may be rendered inoperative by internal factions and schisms, by differences related to goals and means and the pursuit of power. Clashes of personality may highlight differences around pursuing or abandoning previously agreed upon group aims. External pressures can also cause stresses that can lead to decline. Some ex-prisoner groups have found no real outside support, few jobs are forthcoming for members, stigma is high, the group's resources too meager.

Stresses also occur in groups that are by purpose *assertive* and by type of membership *stigmatized*. An international self-help organization like A.A., composed of those who acknowledge their severe handicap, alcoholism, encourages its members to seek to become like everyone else—normal, functioning, coping citizens. Should a group, however, *demand* a place in the sun by insisting upon respect just because of the deviation or stigma of its membership, then, it may face more and more public pressure.

Mixed groups (composed of assertive and assimilative elements) may also encounter internal strains based upon the ambivalence of their members. Edward Sagarin reports that several reasons were offered by those with achondroplasia (hereditary dwarfism) for their nonattendance at meetings of Little People of America: (1) it's a marriage mill—if no further marital and/or love partners can be found, the desire to continue attending meetings rapidly wanes and (2) some feel that the organization forces them to turn inward, despite rhetoric on a national level to the contrary.[7]

In summary then, the degree of congruency with society's norms as well as the extent of the handicap or stigma are probably the two most important criteria for the ability of the group to cope with its internal strains. Additionally, the extent to which the group can go beyond problems of actual survival (maintenance functions) and face up to problems of growth is the crucial indicator of the success of both exchange mechanisms and leadership, despite ongoing internal stress and external pressures.

The Interplay between Ideology and Structure

One possibly significant variable among the groups is that of the intensity and degree of development and strictness of their ideological or theoretical principles. If we place these groups on a

continuum ranging from the more developed and structured ideological beliefs on one hand to those looser and more diffuse on the
other, some interesting derivations may be discerned.

At one extreme, A.A. and Recovery, Inc., are examples of organizations that have a well worked out set of beliefs and derived
practices. They expect and enforce ideological acceptance or
acquiescence and lay down codes of behavior members are expected to follow. The codes set forth are not only connected with
the addiction or problem that the group is combating, but extend
as well to the realm of social behavior. Thus Recovery members
are discouraged from social contacts with other members apart
from the regular meetings.

Meetings of A.A., O.A., and similar groups are rigidly structured; they follow a pattern that encompasses a number of ritualistic elements. Leaders begin by reciting a part of the creed, a
speaker is introduced who uses as a text one of the accepted
writings. This is followed by a patterned general participation
where members ritualistically identify themselves as compulsive
drinkers, overeaters, gamblers, etc., and recount their progress
and vicissitudes since the last meeting.

The get-togethers of Recovery, Inc., follow a different scenario
but are similarly standardized as Lee has shown. After hearing a
speaker or an excerpt from the founder's writings, members describe an incident, relationship, piece of behavior or feeling that
has given them difficulty. The group analyzes this offering using
terms and ideas originated by Dr. Low, and thereby seeks to have
the member reinterpret or perceive the difficulty in a different and
more acceptable way.

This stereotyping of meeting procedures undoubtedly helps
many members of the groups by offering positive reinforcement
for their periods of abstinence or furnishing aid in accepting and
interpreting difficulties they have encountered in everyday living
in the previous period.

It should be emphasized that the kind of responses the group or
other members individually provide in such meetings are circum-
scribed by the organization's beliefs and by the centralized procedures established in expression of them. Spontaneity of reaction
is limited. One can regard such constriction as one of the group's

mechanisms of maintaining its cohesion and as a way of tying members more closely to the organization.

Contrasting with these highly ideologized organizations are those which do not have such a strong set of enforced beliefs and procedures. These may range from a group like Parents Without Partners, bringing together people with a similar life situation and having no stated or conscious ideology, to the Women's Movement, which embraces a startlingly wide range and diversity of ideological currents. It does not seem accidental that the *style* of the latter type of organization is freer and more open to individual variation and influence than in the A.A. type. The style and content of meetings, especially of the consciousness-raising groups in the Women's Movement, are determined by the desires of the participants. There is little stereotyping in approaching conflicts and member participation; the norm appears to be much spontaneity and exchange.

It would be of interest to study the reactions of participant-members at the extremes of such groups, both the highly structured ideological type and the looser variety. Does tightness of structure and enforced belief contribute to stability and maintenance of membership? Is the dropout rate higher in one type than another? And what can be said of membership benefits that might accrue?

Some of the tightly structured groups on the A.A. model expect adherents to remain and never to "graduate" to the wider world. It is one of the organization's tenets that "once a drinker, always a drinker"; reliable control of the problem can only be assured through continued contact with the group. A.A.'s imitators have a similar viewpoint.

The approach of "mixed" or "middle" groups like Parents Without Partners seems to be otherwise; they accept the idea that as their members' circumstances change, they may need or desire no further group contacts. And among the social action groups of which the Women's Movement may be seen as a prototype, there is a noticeable amount of proselytizing. When "liberated" women go out into the community seeking converts to the movement, they attempt to form new small women's groups and new "cells."

These ideological and structural differences relate closely to questions of the dynamics of the various groups' development as well as to the kind of participation they evoke and the benefits members obtain.

Growth and Change in Self-Help Groups

Change is a constant in human institutions, and self-help groups are no exception. They undergo processes of growth, adaptation, decline. Depending on the criteria of judgment, some groups become notable successes, some never fulfill their potential, and some are inevitable failures.

In earlier writings, Alfred Katz[8] formulated a "natural history" of self-help groups, that is, a succession of five "stages" or periods in their development. He cautioned against viewing these as other than abstract and broadly descriptive constructs which overlap in time and characteristics. The stages Katz distinguished are as follows:

1 | Origin

2 | Informal organizational stage

3 | Emergence of leadership

4 | Beginnings of formal organization

5 | Beginnings of professionalization

This formulation arose from a study of a particular kind of self-help group, associations formed by parents of handicapped children. While useful, the scheme applies to some but by no means all of the groups reviewed in this volume. For example, stage five —beginnings of professionalization—is consciously resisted by some of the groups that have been discussed, where resistance to "outside" control, as represented by professionals, is a basic tenet and rationale.

All self-help groups may be said to traverse stages one and two, but stage three—emergence of leadership—does not universally occur. More than a few contemporary groups—the CR (consciousness-raising) units within the Women's Movement and some communes for example—deliberately avoid a designation of leadership. They either remain small enough so that the whole membership makes necessary decisions, or they furnish means for the regular rotation of leadership.

Likewise, stage four—the beginnings of formal organization—may be resisted and never actually reached, especially by smaller, locally oriented and nonproselytizing or nonsocial action groups. Again, some communes and CR groups are examples.

The avoidance of stages four and five provides evidence that Robert Michel's "Iron Law of Oligarchy," which holds that centralization of authority and bureaucratization occur inexorably as organizations grow, does not apply universally to self-help groups on the contemporary scene. Smallness of size, intimacy of interaction, and lack of social action objectives—sometimes coupled to an ideology endorsing shared leadership—characterizes self-help groups that avoid bureaucratic structures.

With the others, however, stages four and five clearly foreshadow and facilitate the growth of bureaucratic machinery and procedures that often contradict the original goals, intent, and styles of self-help aggregates. The dilemma is a continuing one and a source of tension among participants.

Notable examples of already bureaucratized and professionalized groups are of the type originally studied by Katz, where parents came together to bring about more public and professional attention to the problems of their handicapped children. The National Association for Retarded Citizens, the United Cerebral Palsy Association, and many other groups have employed professional staffs, conducted fund-raising campaigns, and are often indistinguishable from conventional philanthropic agencies.

We do not suggest that these organizations could or should have had different careers, or that they are not still helpfully carrying out their original objectives, but it does seem clear that much of their self-help impulses and significance to members has been superseded.

The "Iron Law of Oligarchy" finds its sharpest expression among self-help groups that take this route.

Many examples show that self-help organizations, like voluntary organizations in general, experience difficulty in striking a balance between the conflicting claims of operational effectiveness and participatory democracy. Once they reach a certain level of size and program complexity, self-help groups must carefully consider their future course. The process is complex and unique to every group. The choice is influenced by many things—the nature of the problem confronted, the group's ideology, the support or hostility of the surrounding community. Idiosyncratic and personal differences, especially among leaders, are also important factors. Whichever choice is made—to expand, to "go public" and national, to bureaucratize and professionalize, or to remain small, intimate, nonprofessional—there are gains and losses. Each group thus makes its own decision about its future.

We conclude this part with an excerpt that explores in a different idiom and from another vantage point of analysis some aspects of the dynamics of self-help groups. As a community psychiatrist, Gerald Caplan is interested in how various interpersonal networks provide support for the individual. He discusses a series of these networks—the family, neighborhood "care-givers," and mutual aid groups—in contrasting the acceptability of informal help with that of professionalized agencies.

13

Spontaneous or Natural Support Systems

GERALD CAPLAN

The best-known and most ubiquitous support system in all societies is the marital and family group. Most cultures develop definite rules that legislate the reciprocal obligations that bind kinfolk together, irrespective of their individual feelings about each other, and the more hazardous the ecological situation the more stringent these obligations become, so that people can always rely on being controlled, helped, and guided by their kin whenever they get into difficulties. Likewise, they are obliged to offer similar assistance to other family members whenever the latter are in need, despite the possible personal inconvenience involved.

In our own urban society the effective whittling down of the kinship obligations to the marital couple and the nuclear family is supposed to be compensated for by the development of community caregiving agencies, manned by professionals who are especially skilled in support, and also by the mastery of the environment by urban technology so that individuals are not confronted by many life problems that they must deal with on their own. Clearly, both these implicit assumptions of modern urban society are of questionable validity; and the nuclear family is usually under strain in coping with the consequent frequent demands for support by its members. . . .

The essential elements in a marital or family group . . . acting as a support system are attitudes of sensitivity and respect for the needs of all its members and an effective communication system. It is significant that in most cases where individuals have not been protected from illness and have therefore become accessible to study in our clinics and hospitals, their families have shortcomings in both these aspects. Disorders in marital and parent-child relationships whereby an individual is not perceived as a person in his own right whose idiosyncratic needs are worthy of assessment and satisfaction but serves as a displacement object or scapegoat for vicariously satisfying the needs of other family members are commonplace in our clinical practice. Likewise, disorders of family communication such as double-binds and mystification are a usual finding in our clinical cases. We often think of these distortions of relationship and communication as directly pathogenic, but our present thesis raises the possibility of

SOURCE: A later and expanded version of the ideas in this article appears in *Support Systems and Community Mental Health—Lectures on Concept Development* (New York: Behavioral Publications, 1974), pp. 8-39.

conceptualizing them also as defects in the family support system that failed to protect the individuals from the effects of inadequate feedback in the outside world.

A fascinating reflection on the significance of the family pattern as a basic support system is provided by the frequent finding that individuals who for a variety of reasons do not have a family of their own are often "adopted" by a family to which they are not linked by birth or marriage. This applies not only to children who are formally adopted or fostered, but also to adults. Another version on the same theme has been described by Joan Shapiro in her sensitive study of people living as Single Room Occupants in low-cost rooming houses in New York City.[1] She found that in many of these dilapidated hotels the poverty-stricken inmates spontaneously cluster together in enduring pseudo-family groups, each under the leadership of a dominant woman who acts as a kind of mother who nurtures, guides, and controls those who feel bound to her. Within such a pseudo-family group a network of reciprocal kinlike obligations develops which supports and protects these erstwhile isolated derelicts against the privations of their marginal existence. The familylike groupings among adolescent hippies and dropouts, which sometimes take on a more organized pattern as in the notorious Manson Family, are a similar manifestation, attesting to the attractiveness of the family pattern to people who spontaneously cluster together for mutual support. It is worthy of note that the most frequently verbalized expression by such people of their reason for joining and maintaining their membership in such an aggregate is that in this group they feel that others treat them as unique individuals, try to satisfy their idiosyncratic needs, and support them lovingly in "doing their thing."

In modern English when we wish to refer somewhat poetically to a person's relatives we sometimes use the expression "kith and kin." But in Middle English and Anglo-Saxon this term differentiated between two sets of people. *Kin* denoted those bound by birth or marriage, namely family members. Whereas *kith* denoted friends, acquaintances, and neighbors, giving recognition to the special part played by such people in an individual's life. In its original usage kith represents a support system that is important for many people. This is especially so in our society among members of ethnic subgroups, first- or second-generation immigrants from rural and semirural settlements in Europe.

Kith bonds and supports may be weaker in this country, especially in large cities, than in rural and semirural Europe, but I feel that relatively superficial links with neighbors often do add up to a not insignificant system of supports.

Kin and kith supports mainly provide continuing guidance and direction as well as self-validation. Intermittently they are called into operation to sustain their members in acute crisis situations or in dealing with chronic deprivation. But in confronting such out-of-the-ordinary challenges, kin and kith supports are often augmented by the special services of a network of helping people in the community whom we have named "informal caregivers.". . . When investigating the nature of individual responses to crisis, I found that many individuals in crisis turn to such people for help and guidance and that the outcome of the crisis is much influenced by the quality of their intervention. Robert Liberman[2] made a similar finding when he investigated what appeared to determine whether a mentally ill person entered a mental hospital via a medical referral or via the police. He discovered that of "52 individuals who sought help, 63 percent were influenced by another person in their choice of a particular resource." He found that the people he named "influentials" were older, less likely to be Protestant, more often of a higher socioeconomic class, higher in gregariousness, more stable residentially, and more likely to have had prior experience with mentally ill family members than those who sought their guidance. . . .

An in-depth study of such informal caregivers . . . is long overdue, but meanwhile my impressions of them include the following: they are of two types, "generalists" and "specialists." The "generalists" are likely to be people who are widely recognized in their neighborhood to have wisdom in matters of human relations or to be knowledgeable about the community caregiving system. As Liberman pointed out, they are gregarious; that is, they make easy contacts and like to involve themselves with other people. Often, they have a social or economic role that brings them into repetitive contact with many others; for instance, they may serve in a drugstore or a grocery store, or they may be hairdressers, bartenders, policemen, or newspaper vendors. Often they have had emotional problems themselves or have had to deal with such difficulties in their own families, and this has stimulated their interest and understanding. Some of them may appear to us to be currently disturbed and to be trying to master their own problems vicariously by intervening in the lives of others, but it is my impression that if they consistently give ineffectual advice they soon get a bad name in their locality and people stop paying attention to them.

. . . The "specialist" counselors are rather different. They are usually people who are known to have suffered some misfortune or to have undergone a particular trying experience and to have worked out ways of achieving a successful adjustment and adaptation. Their personality gifts and interest in helping others may be of less significance than the quality of their adaptation and their demonstration of mastery over their own life difficulties, at least as this is perceived by the people around them. They are sought out by others who find themselves in the same boat and they are asked for their advice as people who have personal experience of this problem. Eventually, some of these people who have successfully handled their own predicament and have subsequently been asked to help others with similar difficulties discover that they enjoy this kind of service, and both they and the people who turn to them for help find that they have some interpersonal talent. They may then develop a local reputation as a helpful person, and many fellow sufferers may turn to them and may be given guidance and support.

The variety of such specialized local informal helpers is large; almost anyone with an illness or disability, or exposed to a personal or family predicament or challenge has a tendency to seek guidance from somebody else who has traveled a similar experiential route. . . . Our Harvard group has been informally studying this phenomenon for several years. When . . . we were conducting our research on adjustment of parents to the birth of a premature baby, we were impressed by the number who actively sought advice from other parents who had earlier been through the same experience. . . . There was a positive correlation between making a special effort to look for such information from other parents and a healthy adaptation to the crisis.[3] It appeared that information about what to expect and how to treat the baby was obtained in a more understandable and usable form from other parents than from the professionals, despite the latter's more standardized expertise and wider experience. We found similar patterns of seeking guidance from people with prior personal experience among the parents of babies with congenital defects and with mental retardation. But the best example of the phenomenon was the case of widows. My colleague Phyllis Silverman conducted a survey of recently widowed women in order to discover whom they had found to be most helpful to them at different phases of their bereavement. She reported that

> *Most caregivers shy away from the bereaved. Widows I have talked with felt that neither friends, family, physicians, nor clergymen, for that matter, were very helpful. All wanted them to recover as quickly as possible. On the other hand, they found that other widows could be extremely helpful; they were least likely to tell them to "keep a stiff upper lip" at a time when the widows felt their lives were ended and any hope for the future gone. Other widows realized that grief was temporary and had to run its course before it was possible to feel better again.[4]*

So other widows would encourage them to weep and would weep along with them, utilizing this as an opportunity to continue, although at a much lower intensity, their unending process of mourning for their own dead spouse. The new widows felt that the veteran widows really understood their situation, as no nonwidowed person could, and that what they said was authentic because it was based on personal experience.

The outstanding characteristic of these informal caregivers, both generalists and specialists, is that they are nonprofessionals. They are amateurs in the fullest sense of the word.

Webster defines an amateur as "a person who does something for the pleasure of it rather than for money; nonprofessional; hence, a person who does something more or less unskillfully."[5] While it is true that compared with professionals whose performance is supposed to be standardized at a high level of skill by appropriate recruitment, training, and supervision, these amateur caregivers are quite varied; many of them are just as effective in their supportive achievements as professionals and some of them get better results because of their amateur status. For instance, the informal caregivers usually do not maintain a professional-style distance and objectivity in dealing with the people they help. . . . They do not empathize, rather they identify. All this adds up to a direct person-to-person influence that has an authenticity and spontaneity that is rare among professionals except among those who are the best trained and the most talented.

Another characteristic of informal caregivers is that there is a mutual and reciprocal quality in their interactions with the people they help. The giver and receiver of support are equally, though differently, benefited by the contact. This is especially obvious in the case of a veteran giving counsel to a recent sufferer, when the former plays an active role in a situation that revives in him the memory of an experience in which previously he himself was the relatively passive sufferer, so that he may now exercise mastery in place of his former victimization. This is made all the more vivid because he vicariously reexperiences the old pains and discomforts as he identifies with the current sufferer. This identification is overtly or covertly recognized by the sufferer, and it is because of this recognition that he feels so well understood. . . . In such contacts neither party is standardized, so they do not need to feel that they are "cases" and therefore, to some extent, "put down." While the interaction of professional and client is hierarchical, that of the amateur supporter and the person he is helping coordinate . . . is usually entirely voluntary on both sides; and the absence of financial payment makes it seem a more sincere and personalized service that is energized by true loving-kindness.

Organized Supports Not Directed by Caregiving Professionals

The second main category of supports are those that are organized through formal groups and associations which are established and maintained by people similar to the informal caregivers we have just described. These organizations sometimes use caregiving professionals as resource people. If they are big enough, they may use professional administrators or other paid professional staff, but the main direction remains in the hands of the amateurs. There are two types of such organizations, the voluntary service groups and the mutual help groups.

A good contemporary example of such a volunteer service organization is the one initiated in 1964 in London by a group of young people under the leadership of a twenty-seven-year-old barrister, Anthony Steen. Within four years he and a group of like-minded young people, all in their twenties, built up an organization of more than 10,000 volunteers between the ages of fourteen and thirty, who devoted themselves to serving the lonely and elderly people of London. They called their organization Task Force, and they captured the imagination of young people of all classes throughout the city. Their members conducted a house-to-house search for lonely old people and put these in touch with volunteers prepared to give companionship and immediate help, such as redecorating rooms, window cleaning, shopping, repairing radio and television sets, pushing wheelchairs, playing cards, hairdressing, shaving, sewing and mending, and taking them to the movies or for car outings. Most important, many of the young volunteers built ongoing relationships with the elderly as proxy-grandchildren, and they also brought many of the old people together into small peer groups.

The volunteers organized and staffed their own offices in seven of the London boroughs and linked up with the municipal health and welfare services. They actively recruited other volunteers from among senior schoolchildren, university students, and in industry, as well as from churches and recreational organizations. Their success was recognized by the British government, and in 1968 a countrywide Voluntary Community Service by Young People was established along similar lines, with the support of several government ministries.[6]

Our own Peace Corps, VISTA, and local youth organizations, such as Harvard's Philips Brooks House, and many other associations of student volunteers who serve in mental hospitals, nursing homes, settlement houses, and in outreach services to the underprivileged, are too well known to need more than a brief mention. Perhaps less well known to a mental health audience, but undeservedly, is the volunteer service effort of people at the other end of the age scale, the American Association of Retired Persons, which currently has a membership of 3.5 million and which in addition to its mutual help activities harnesses the tremendous energy of its countrywide membership in a wide range of local and regional service projects. It would be hard to find another organization that so aptly demonstrates the mutuality of the benefit to helper and helped in activities that provide the opportunity for retired people to continue to fulfill themselves in useful service to individuals, organizations, and the general community.

The second type of supportive organizations are the mutual help associations. Some of these have a long history. The Freemasons, for instance, was started in the Middle Ages after the Black Death had devastated Europe and destroyed much of society's supportive structure. The organization had previously been a craft guild of stonemasons, but as a response to the perils and privations of the times, it reorganized to build a social matrix for its members to support them in withstanding the confusions of their environment. . . .

Similar organizations have emerged to support population subgroups whenever there has been rapid cultural change or social disorganization, for instance, in countries experiencing massive immigration, the newcomers often band together in *landsmanshaften* or ethnic organizations, and in "fraternal" associations such as Elks, Lions, Workingmen's Club, and the like. The veterans organizations that grow up after wars are another example. In addition to providing a range of acceptable social activities in familiar surroundings, most of these organizations establish group insurance against sickness and death and traditions of helping each other in times of personal need both by financial loans and by mutual counseling as well as by visiting the sick and bereaved.

Supplementing such "generalist" organizations, we also find mutual help associations that are the collective analogues of the individual specialized caregivers, namely organizations of people who have all suffered a particular disability or undergone a challenging experience, and which provide a structure for mutual support in withstanding deprivations or for old-timers to help the recent additions to their ranks. The best-known example of this type of organization in our own days is Alcoholics Anonymous. . . .

Alcoholics Anonymous was in part a reaction against the ineffectiveness of professional treatment of alcoholics, what today we would call a counter-culture. The current increase in drug abuse and the widespread disenchantment with formal professional treatment programs has stimulated the emergence of a host of self-help groups organized by ex-addicts. Matthew Dumont[7] has written a thoughtful study of this phenomenon. One of his most interesting findings is . . . that the atmosphere in many of these self-help groups is explicitly authoritarian. Members are expected to adhere to a strict code of conduct, centering of course on drug abstinence. They are kept under careful surveillance, and they are severely judged for backsliding, which is punished by public condemnation and shaming. On the other hand, if they keep the rules and demonstrate commitment to the social norms and traditions of the group, they are progressively elevated in status until they are admitted to the top leadership stratum, and in their turn may command the respect and obedience of those lower in the hierarchy. Dumont uses the term "paramilitary" in describing the controls and sanctions of the ex-addict organizations.

To me they also resemble religious orders in their social structure and controls. All these institutions have in common a well-defined mission to train members and support them in a disciplined new style of life; and they combine an authoritarian hierarchy with an open-ended upward mobility system that balances punitive sanctions for nonconformity with the very tangible rewards of unlimited promotion for merit. They differ fundamentally from professional care systems in that the latter maintain a rigid boundary between the lay clients and the professional staff, and no amount of egalitarian nonjudgmentalism ever completely obscures the essential "put down" involved.

Organizations that help their members break a noxious habit—alcoholism, drug abuse, smoking, or overeating—offer not only individual and group counseling in dealing with the problems involved, and particularly anticipatory guidance from old-timers in preparing for expectable difficulties, but they also extend individual ego strength by group sharing of the miseries and discomforts of withdrawal symptoms. In addition, they provide a community in which friendships can develop to provide a new meaning to life, and social and recreational activities can take place that offer a distraction from the unsatisfied cravings.

Another group of organizations places its main emphasis on the provision of a new community in which members may immerse themselves. These are the organizations catering to those who have suffered a major loss or relatively unalterable disability or deprivation, such as Parents Without Partners, widows associations, parents of mentally retarded or psychotic children, mastectomy and ileostomy associations, amputees, disabled war veterans, and the like. Most of these self-help groups have two-phase programs. The old-timers help the new members to master the trauma of the acute crisis of the bereavement, the loss of bodily integrity, or the disappointment of parental hopes by individual and group counseling and by emotional support in expressing and mastering the shock and pain, as well as by guidance in accepting and coming to terms with the catastrophe. But the characteristic feature of these organizations is their second phase provision of long-term social contacts and joint activities to serve as a kind of psychosocial replacement for what has been lost.[8] This never really works—no amount of friendliness in meetings of Parents Without Partners can replace the intimacy of a marital relationship, nor can collaborating with other parents in bettering the lot of the mentally retarded make up for the lifelong feeling of emptiness caused by having a child who will never develop to continue the chain of one's life. But at least the association with others in the same boat combats the social isolation that would otherwise be the lot of those who feel themselves and are perceived by others to be deviant in ordinary society.

A characteristic feature of many of the organizations of the deprived is that they develop cohesion and some sense of mastery over cruel fate by campaigning politically to improve the community's handling of the needs of people like themselves.

The outstanding example of this has been the activism of associations of parents of the retarded, who have been extremely successful in forcing the authorities to provide radical improvements in the care of their children. In the process they have emerged from their previous shame-burdened obscurity and ineffectuality to powerful roles on the community stage that have given them self-respect and a deeply meaningful experience of channeling their frustrated nurturance into a useful cause. . . .

Part IV

Against the
"Mainstream":
Therapy and
Politics in
Dissenting
Communities

. . . Is it not possible that these organizations are an expression of a wider movement that has taken hold in this country, a demand for control by people over their own lives and their own fate? It is populism and grass roots in a new form. Self-help is Mississippi and SNCC and freedom schools; it is hippies and cop-outs and Haight-Ashbury as much as it is Illegitimates Anonymous and Vanguard and an organization of epileptics.

—Edward Sagarin

In Part II we reviewed and attempted to order in a classification scheme the large, varied, and sometimes confusing array of contemporary self-help groups.

In addition to differing in their predominant focus of concern and activity, we suggested that self-help groups differ along another important axis—whether they accept or conform to the normative and accepted values of the dominant groups and institutions of society, the so-called mainstream, or whether they resist and oppose them.

Part IV discusses groups whose relationship to "mainstream" values is a critical and explicit element of their purposes, styles, and inner life.

The article on Operation Bootstrap is based on a series of tape-recorded interviews with Lou Smith, one of Bootstrap's founders and continuing leaders.

Warren Haggstrom's projection of a grass-roots model of local community-organizing also bears upon the possibilities, conditions, and constraints of setting up viable structures that, while seeing themselves as "outside the Establishment," may seek to influence and modify it.

Janet Norman's account of consciousness-raising underlines the place of self-help in perhaps the widest and potentially the most important social phenomenon of our time—the Women's Movement.

I'm trying to give you how all these things come together. There's no one instant. There's an instant when you make a decision, but it comes out of long lines of experiences.

14

Operation Bootstrap
LOU SMITH

Bootstrap's History

Operation Bootstrap technically got started toward the tail end of the Watts revolt. I was then still Western Regional Director for CORE [Congress of Racial Equality] and then there was Robert Hall with Envac, the civil rights organization in Los Angeles—a spin-off of the old CORE chapter —and we knew that our civil rights movement, as we knew it, was over. I and Stokely [Carmichael], who was with SNCC [Student Nonviolent Coordinating Committee], and most of the other guys, had suspicions it was over after the Democratic National Convention at Atlantic City when we had gotten together and were sold out by Johnson-Humphrey. That Freedom party was a beautiful thing—the spirit was there and we built something. I remember Wayne Morse came out on the boardwalk and explained to us how they were taking the delegates away—and how Humphrey had been commissioned to stop this threat which was the only big threat at the Democratic convention of that year. Edith Green, congresswoman from Oregon, came out too and they explained that we had enough delegates to seat the Freedom party, but Humphrey was going from delegation to delegation saying that they would lose all political patronage if they went with the party and not with the compromise. Everybody was gearing up to Goldwater you see and Humphrey's vice-presidency hinged on the deals made in that room.

So afterward all of us in CORE went up to Nyack, New York, the birthplace of CORE, the Fellowship of Reconciliation Hall. We did some soul-searching and commissioned Jim Farmer, who was then head of Congress on Racial Equality, to write a position paper on where he thought the movement and the organization should go, and to present it at the next CORE convention. That convention was held at Durham, North Carolina, June/July 1965. Jim Farmer wrote something that to me was monumental, it was called "The Black Ghetto, the Awakening Giant." He wrote that, though it was important that we'd won the freedom rides, had this sit-in movement, and took down "white only" signs, he had a feeling that we had left the ghettos and run off into the hinterlands and our own house was about to burn. He wrote the whole article on how the civil rights movement should now return to their home bases and start cleaning up the Harlems and the Chicagos. That was in July 1965, and I came away from that convention in time to get back to Los Angeles and—Watts burned. Just when Jim had been talking about these things this community blew up.

Then it occurred to me that here was a big CORE organization sitting in Los Angeles that had been sending the people to the marches in Selma, and all that kind of bullshit and it hadn't taken care of homework. We really began looking at our community and what it needed and out of that we got an idea.

I had been at war with CORE over some tendency within the organization to go the "poverty" route. Will Ussery, the first vice-chairman, was an advocate of that. He was in San Francisco, I was in Los Angeles, and we used to debate hours into the night. I kept telling Will that I didn't believe that this government would finance its own overthrow. I was now feeling that we had to get back onto the streets and start building our home base. Will said no, that the government was going to be spending billions of dollars in this poverty thing and we'd better get our hands on it and direct it—the same old game of thinking that you can direct that money. But I couldn't conceive of that money really being used for the benefit of the black community. Well, anyway, Will went on and built the thing on Fillmore Street (in San Francisco) and we started Bootstrap. We started out just with the idea—we were going to use the inventiveness and ingenuity of the black community—some of what the movement was talking about. From there we didn't know where we were going.

The first thing we built was a welfare recipients' unit where we could start giving out some food and clothing, a little community center where people could come and we'd sit around and rap. From there we evolved into a job training center—because people around needed jobs and they were screaming they needed skills. So we had one of the best job training centers in this city, and we didn't have a nickel. We hustled keypunch machines from IBM and had 360 computer time donated from Systems Development Corporation.

We turned out a helluva lot of good students, but then two things were soon obvious: One, there wasn't a question of job training—and something kept sticking in my mind—the only time I had been on the West Coast was in 1963—and this is the freakishness of it all! I'd never been west of the Mississippi River, and in 1963, CORE held a National Action Council meeting and we were going to hold it in Los Angeles and I was in Philadelphia—

Jim Farmer was in New York—we were all supposed to meet in Los Angeles. I went down to Philadelphia airport that morning in time to get breakfast and who should be eating breakfast there but Jim Farmer. We got on the plane together and we came west. We came to Los Angeles. Somehow over the Rocky Mountains I remember Jim told me—he said, "Lou, I got a brainstorm! I know how to mess this country up." And I said, "What's that, Jim?" He said, "Let's train all the unemployed and dump them on the labor market and then ask them, '*Now,* what's your excuse?' " We laughed about it you know, and I thought then it was kind of revolutionary—it makes you then confront that bullshit of "it's only a matter of training." And that was sticking in my mind.

Second, I also knew that the "guilt" money was starting to dry up. After we didn't burn the second and third year, donations began to fall off. Then it became obvious that we had to build our own economic base. We had to build things that were going to give us our own income that we could use as we wanted to, otherwise we'd have to go the Sargent Shriver route—the poverty program. By that time Will Ussery's thing in San Francisco was failing, the mayor took it over and they had a board of directors. They can control those indigenous community boards because you find very few people at the street level who are politically sophisticated enough to deal with the jargon and the methods of the slick politicians. They'll take your nitty-gritty, very honest, moralistic people and sit them down in a room and convince them that they're right. It sounds good, but it's sort of like the Indian— you know, thinking he was making treaties, but they ended up with no country.

So we made several attempts. We started a little sewing factory that made Afro garments and it worked out very well, but we looked at that and saw we'd never be over twelve to fifteen people anyway. So we let that ride and tried gas stations, all that kind of thing . . . and then this came along.

All the time mulling in our minds was the idea we needed to really start working with job training in the sense that you build industries and then train people where they can get paid while they're going through training, and you can do all these other things we wanted. You could do *much* better than sitting trying to run somebody through a training program. Because you got to deal with the whole person—it's not just the lack of skills, it's the lack of self-confidence that had settled in that I found was more destructive. Ironically, it was a white woman, Ruth Warrick, an actress, who really opened us up to that. The first class we ever had at Bootstrap was in communication skills, where people sat around in a circle and started learning to talk to each other and that role-playing thing, and so forth. We found out something interesting—that the entire class except one (thirteen people were in it) went off and got jobs on their own, before we even got equipment to start doing job training. And all she had done, through all those interactions, was to help to build the confidence of the individuals to the point where they could take care of their own business. That's when we got very, very interested in this whole interaction thing. At that time, remember, going along in concert with that, was the whole move of the black community from "Black Is Beautiful" to little kids putting out the newspaper "Black Is Back" (the Black Students Union at Thomas Jefferson High School). For the first time we were starting to use the word *black*. But before 1965 if you called someone black they'd knock your teeth out. Black was a fighting word then. I wasn't really sure what was going on, but I could see it because it was happening in me too—I was moving myself from self-hatred toward self-love.

. . . I'd begun to notice how, as people got more confidence in themselves as individuals and more confident with the black thing, there was less demand for job training and more demand for total change in this society, and then more interest in instead-of-asking-*me*-to-help-*you*—*you*-would-help-*yourself* type of thing. I think I understand a lot of it now, but at that time. . . .

Then along came three guys from Mattel—the owner, the general manager, and the vice-president in charge of marketing. They came down and presented us with a proposal—the way they put it was that they thought it was time that they, as a giant corporation, got involved in social problems in the community, and they also said that they had been looking around at all organizations, checking them out, and the Bootstrap philosophy fitted closest to theirs. The way they put it to me and Robert Hall that day was: "If we could help you do something what would you want us to do, knowing what kind of business we're in." Well, the first thing that hit me right up the back was black dolls—because I'd always remembered that can of crap thing where they took black kids and gave them black dolls and white dolls and the kids chose the white dolls. That was all part of that self-hatred—at that time I was deep into that—going through it myself—from self-hatred to self-love—you know I always felt I could do better because I was lighter skinned and I was taught that way as a kid. . . . So they said, "O.K. you'll hear from us," and they just left.

You know, I've been through these things a million times. I never expected to hear from them, but one day we got called to Mattel. We went over there, and here was the deal they wanted to make: They would put up all the initial capital, they would do all the training and put in all the equipment. Our job would be to select the people that were going to be trained and to select the site and to design the kind of dolls we wanted to make. We wouldn't pay them back any money. It would be an outright gift from them to us. They would not own any of the factory, which they couldn't by law anyhow because we have no stockholders. We'd be a nonprofit corporation and they couldn't own it. We said, "That sounds good." They said they would stay with us no matter how long it took, and they estimated it would take two to two and one half years for us to get to about a $200,000–$250,000 a year concern.

I like to talk about this because it's the highlight of my life. I *had* to make a decision—not over the deal, because we had nothing to lose. That sounded like the kind of thing we wanted to get into. But sitting there with them—I had walked picket lines at Mattel—primarily for their war-toy bit—I don't know, something was gnawing at me. When things are gnawing me, I find it's better to get 'em the hell off my chest rather than go home and say I wish I hadn't. I've done too much wishing—I had all my life and I figure I don't have to do that no more. So here we are sitting across the table from all these big brass—and they handed us this deal—and I just told them, I said, "Well, it sounds good but there's one thing we've got to have understanding on—this has nothing to do with my right to attack you publicly or privately or however I please for your making of war toys." Then, boy! poor Robert Hall, I heard him stop breathing—I stopped breathing. For a minute that room got so quiet you could hear a rat piss on the carpet. And I expected to hear them say, "Well, fuck you, you little ungrateful bastard," you know—or something. I forget who was the first but somebody broke the silence by starting to talk about the whole issue of war toys—how they were trying to phase them out and then they got to the whole thing of it. They brought out the first little machine gun that they made which was very popular and so forth and so on and they understood, and the agreement was kicked off.

Now, I found out later, there was more to it than that. What happened was Cliff Jacobs, vice-president in charge of marketing, and his crazy brother Paul, whom we love very much, were having dinner with the Handlers, the owners of Mattel, one day when Paul was in town. And the Handlers threw out an idea that what they wanted to do to help the black community was to come down and put a plant in Watts off of Mattel. And they tell me that Paul Jacobs jumped up from the table and said, "Now that's just what the fuck the black community needs, another missionary and exploiting outfit to come down here and set up a plant." So they tell me the Handlers said, "Well, what the hell *do* they want?" and Paul said, "Well, if you want to do anything worth a damn, it would seem to me that you'd go down and help them build their own damn plant and get out." And that's how the idea came about. But we didn't know about that until later.

At that time the funds had just practically dried up. We were existing off hustling just to pay the rent. The job training end was just becoming nonexistent, and yet you train a couple of classes and there ain't no jobs and you don't have the guts to go out and tell people to come back in and train some more. So our whole Bootstrap dream was getting the shit kicked out of it and we were diminishing as an organization down into a hard-core group of people who still believed that the raw talent was there on the streets. And so we turned into this.

Despite lack of business know-how, we grossed in our first

year, to the surprise of everybody, $300,000 in sales (Mattel
thought it'd take us two to two and one half years to get to
$250,000) but lost about as much.

Mattel helped us immeasurably in putting out the first doll,
Baby Nancy. The way we got our dolls—we went to all the high
schools and we had kids draw up the kinds of dolls they wanted
and out of this we selected Baby Nancy.

Where Mattel couldn't help us is that they had grown so big
that they had lost the concept of what it is like to be in the garage
(where the Handlers had started). The people they were sending
over to help us had only known big business methods. Our idea
was that the damn plant manager should be out there on that
floor, but *they* talked him into building two offices, one for him
and one for his secretary, air-conditioning and all that kind of
foolishness.

We made some drastic mistakes, but anyway we learned from
that. It was a hard experience, our overhead was too high—that's
the way we got to learn what overhead means. And damn it if we
didn't get mad because all we could see was that we were providing jobs for about thirty people, but we certainly were not anywhere near getting any resources to build the kind of things we
wanted to build. And we were pretty frustrated, so we sat down
and had a real soul-searching and said, goddammit, in the second
year we're going to do different.

We still have problems with bureaucracy. The management is
our weakest link, but the production line people—it's a whole
story in itself. How the negative image has changed. They
thought it would just be a temporary job. When they first came to
work for an all-black firm, they still had the image that niggers
couldn't do nothing.

After we survived the first year and then Mattel helped us get
financing from a bank, we were on our own. We tightened our
belts, man, and we turned this muddle around from the $300,000
loss in the first year. In the second year we doubled sales to about
$600,000 and to all intents and purposes we broke even. We did
some very, very conservative bookkeeping and we held a lot of
stuff out, and it showed on the books as a small loss. Which blew
the bankers' minds—they didn't think that we could turn around

that way. This is now our third year, I think we'll come in somewhere between a million and one half and two million. We'll make enough money to where we can stand up without any donations.

Bootstrap's Future and Philosophy

We keep saying Bootstrap was to be self-sustaining and not depend on anyone else. That's why we're going to get into this whole child-care thing. We want to do education as well, which you can't call "school" because then you go under the state board.

One of the problems in this community is that the whole economic thing is closed in so tight that the parent doesn't ever get a chance. We need to relieve the parents so they have freedom to work if they need to work during the day. Then the parent can give their love instead of frustration. Somewhere around 70 percent of the people who work in this plant have young kids. When we jump off into what we call just a day-care center, these people can be the first to bring their kids to work. We have a strong suspicion that's going to help the whole morale of the plant and attendance.

We want to expand it beyond just the plant, but we're going to start out right here and we also know that once we go down that road we have made a commitment to build all the way to a university.

Just the general direction—we know we've got to have competent medical care. That is where expertise comes in. We're also going to need somebody who knows about diets, for children and for nursing mothers. I also think there should be a school of law, because law is different in these ghettos than in that other world. There's a different type of law and there are different ways of maneuvering around that they don't learn in the regular way.

We get an idea and we've got to try to do it. This whole thing is still in conception, and we don't know what the hell we're doing, but we know what needs to be done. We're going to jump in there just like we did here. We're going to experiment and try everything we know.

In this society whether we like it or whether we don't, if these kids are really going to make it—by making it, I mean at least they can come to the point where they can find the basics—they are going to need expertise. One of the basics is they're going to need to know how to read. A kid's self-confidence is going to have to be built up at a very early age, long before school. The longer you wait the harder it is.

We can't use professionals. We are not going outside to get the people. We are going to hire people from among our own. The worst thing in this world we can do is get people from a different class. But people are going to need at least some background training. We're talking about turning kids on, not just baby-sitting. The system is turning out some very, very insensitive teachers. We've been looking at the kibbutz in Israel and at Montessori, and somewhere in between those ideas are the techniques we want.

We want to build that school system because we want an alternative to what is out there, so that people can at least see. You know, it's one thing to be able to say it and look at figures and realize it, but it's another thing when we bring our three- and four-year-olds and compare 'em with the school system's nine-, ten-, and eleven-year-olds out of the same community. Then they can never again tell us it's genetic.

We just hope that by that time there's enough pressure being built up in the school system itself. We want the example to be the battering ram, our lever, the example of these kids right off the same block with the kids the school system's been fucking with, and we're going to *use* that. We're going to use that as a hammer and we want every other living and swinging kid to use it as a hammer.

Our ultimate hope is that we can phase out of the *business*, because the society itself will begin to realize that any society that doesn't use its potential, that throws away its future like we're throwing it away—not only with these black kids on the corner but also with white middle-class kids, driving them up walls—can't survive. You see you can't survive by throwing away that kind of talent.

Personally, I'd just like to follow just one class of those kids from their mothers' bellies through that university and I think that then if I've got the drive to survive that long—and if it takes twenty-five years I don't give a damn—at the end of that my personal life will have been worthwhile.

And it gets more personal than that. I was declared ineducable in the twelfth grade, you see, and I still got hang-ups of that so I'm doing this a lot from very selfish points of view. I have to overcome a whole lot of negativeness in me, and these kids come from what I come from—the corner on the welfare, and I'm going to get my immortality through that.

We feel that we can build anything now. We're gaining confidence in this economic world. We know right from the plant that the slave masters, if they'd had any sense at all, could have got ten times the work out of us by not whipping us. That's living proof out there in our plant. You know, you don't whip 'em and they work hard, and everybody when they've finished their work they go and help other people do it—that's what's making it work right now.

To show you how badly brainwashed we are, right here in this plant, we developed almost a class thing between the so-called front and the back. We just busted that. The tendency has been to hire people who *look* like they would fit in the front and who *look* like they'd fit into the back. But the best talent we got is out on the floor and our most fucked-up is in the front. Then it'd just stand to reason to start moving people up from the back and they can make the front like they made the back and they'll be the future managers of all the enterprises we ever get into. I feel that everybody in this plant now could run this place.

I found out that when you *allow* people to grow, you grow. Versus trying to *drive* people to grow. You're only going to drive me as far up that tree as you made it uncomfortable for me underneath, and if you ain't careful I'm liable to get mad and drop right off the tree and kick your ass. In the long run you're not going to get anything out of it. How do we expect to beat giants who are out there already with tons of money? Unless we got our spirit, to have something more than the material things—we got to keep alive the spirit. So if somebody has a birthday we hold a party right here in the warehouse.

Just allow people to grow, and I found out that "the way a

business has to run'' is a bunch of crap. I find that more and more of our kids who come here who got business ideas are beginning to find that this may very well be the economics of the future.

I do know that you've got to have economics, no matter what kind of system you've got. If I see anything in this system so far that's wrong, it's that money is allowed to make money. I think a person should be allowed to climb as high as he can, but I don't think you should be able to take money and then from there on into perpetuity invest your money and make money. I think that if money is going to be made it should come from each person's initiative, talent. At the same time we should develop a floor below which *no* competitor can fall—I mean food, shelter, clothing, good medical care, and education should be available for everybody. . . . We're just trying to prove—the idea of Bootstrap —that with no real bosses, where people can do their things—you get screwed a lot and you make a lot of mistakes, but I look at the other rigid organizations and they get screwed more and they make more mistakes—we're still hanging in there. We've invested these three years just for learning and now. . . .

15

Power and Collective Self-Help

WARREN C. HAGGSTROM

There is little agreement among experts about how many Americans are poor. But it is clear that poverty is not closely related to mere deprivation of access to resources. In seventeenth-century England, where resource deprivation was severe by today's standards, it was estimated that *one*-fifth of the population were "paupers."[1] A 1962 publication of the Conference on Economic Progress in the United States estimated that poverty and deprivation affected two-fifths of the nation.[2] Leonard Freedman has written that there is agreement at least that the poor are a minority in the United States. He continues:

> *The size of this minority is subject to dispute: The federal government estimates it as close to 20 percent; some conservatives insist that it is around 10 percent; whereas Leon Keyserling and others have argued that, if we included those living in "deprivation" as well as unalloyed economic misery, over 35 percent of our population suffer from obvious material insufficiency.*[3]

If one divides American society between the affluent and those not affluent who are regarded as poor, the statistics dispute even Freedman's postulated consensus. By this definition, we might regard a majority of families in the United States as poor in 1970.[4]

Since scientists and statisticians have merely operationalized various commonsense notions of poverty, it is in principle impossible to make a precise and valid estimate of the number of Americans who are poor. For the purposes of the following discussion we will merely suppose, with most experts, that the poor are some substantial minority of the American population.

Can Lowest-Income People Be Organized?

By reputation, lowest-income people are least organizable for the exercise of power. Included are those with work that pays very little, people occasionally employed or employed as migratory farm workers. They also include people in public mental institutions, in places for the indigent aged, in prisons, in "convalescent homes." This reputation is also shared by subsistence farmers, skid-row residents, "welfare recipients," public housing residents, and so forth.

It used to be said also that migratory farm workers in California could not organize because of the power of the growers, the availability of alternative imported Mexican labor, and the transient nature of the work force. Now, as the farm workers' organization is affiliated with the AFL-CIO, those arguments no longer convince so many people.

Neighborhood economic and political organization is more difficult. It is not easy to locate viable organizations of the lowest-income people on a neighborhood basis. One problem that has not been worked out is that of an adequate funding of such organizations. Yet *our experience suggests that most of the lowest-income people can create effective, power-directed democratic self-help organizations.* The remainder of this report illustrates aspects of such a process.

The Process of Organization

First, a population is selected. Usually it is comprised of a thousand or more adults in enough proximity to one another to attend common meetings and who can be mobilized around a variety of issues. The population need not be homogeneous by age or ethnicity or initial interest. It should be one which can define rather quickly a number of problems that can be solved through collective action on its own behalf.

Initially defined problems need not seem important to researchers or other strangers. For example, a social scientist may see as most fundamental for some population, defective family structures, unfortunate parental attitudes toward education, or a general failure to use existing services effectively. The people themselves may be more concerned with the failure of the police to protect and serve them, the dangerous neighborhood railroad tracks where children play, or the apparently capricious vagaries of public welfare decisions. The people will organize only around what *they* regard as problems and will be indifferent or hostile toward alternative definitions.

Second, an organizer begins to talk with members of the population to help them define their problems and to illustrate how people elsewhere have overcome similar obstacles through forming themselves into organizations.

After initial individual conversations with the organizer, people are helped to hold small or large meetings in which they gradually achieve a consensus about their situation and problems, the nature of the organization which they might build, and short-term and longer-range objectives. The initial consensus is fragile, that is, beginning to crystallize social reality different from that in which they have lived. A few weeks or months after the organizer initially contacts the people, the latter hold a large meeting to decide whether to create an organization powerful enough to secure changes that are wanted and cannot otherwise be obtained. In most such cases the people decide to organize and are helped by the organizer to create an appropriate decision-action structure for their purpose. Over time, the organizer increasingly finds himself working in a reality created, and in an organization run, by the people. He is necessary to that world, but does not dominate it. His participation is analogous to that of a janitor in an office building or a parliamentarian in a legislative body.

The process of beginning organization, abstractly described above, can break down in a variety of ways. The population may decide to organize, but not to pay the cost of an expanding organizational effort. This necessary cost includes a salary for the organizer, some contribution to support the education of additional organizers, and some support for the creation of additional organizations of low-income people. All these costs are essential to the building of power. Were the organization to depend on conventional outside funding sources, those sources would tend to become shakier as organizational effort became more effective. Any new and independent political force will be attacked by the political status quo; any deliberate and massive shift in buying patterns will be attacked by the economic status quo. In either case, government and foundation funds provide a risky basis for the security of an organizational effort planned to secure social change through the exercise of power.

Key members of an organization, together with a competent organizer, keep things together by establishing norms of solidarity, by ensuring that the organization visibly accomplishes things important to the members, by thinking through the outcomes of various proposals being made, by developing a clear distinction between disagreement on issues and personal attacks, by clearly distinguishing agreement on issues from cronyism, by becoming clear about the difference between symbolic protest gestures and the development of power to force social change.

Given the present level of knowledge, we know how to ensure that most designated very-low-income populations will actively engage themselves in the process of organization creation, although the problem of developing enough funding from low income populations is as yet only partly solved.

Organization of Lowest-Income People: Maintenance

The self-help organizations described in the present report are concerned with the exercise of power. Power-oriented organizations require a more complex structure than that which is necessary to organizations concerned solely with the mobilization of public opinion and organizational maintenance. Power-oriented organizations of low-income people seek to assemble *all* the legitimate motivations and skills in their populations. Such organizations divide up activities, assigning a multiplicity of tasks simultaneously to many kinds of people who are skilled and who will work to carry them out. One committee may concern itself with voter registration, voter education, and swing bloc voting. Another may tackle consumer education and selective buying. Committees may occupy themselves with fashion shows, fish fries, housing demonstrations, planning and research on recreation and leisure, public welfare changes, police activities, improvement of education, libraries, jobs, gardening, or any other present or future concerns.

As much as possible of a population is thereby drawn into a complex organization guided by its general membership. As people involve themselves in nonpower activities of the organization, they become identified with the organization and its programs. For example, people who are at first interested in scenic tours sponsored by the organization end up supporting the organization in its recommendations concerning voting, selective buying, or other power-related actions.

The complexity of structure of power-oriented organizations carries along with it special problems. It necessitates a high degree of skill and energy in coordination, communication, task education, and other aspects usually found under the label "administration." In practice, these complexities require the permanent attention of competent full-time organizers. Let us here consider only two of the complications that require the contributions made by such organizers.

One is the problem of maintaining the democracy of the organization, of making certain that neither the leaders nor the organizer but rather the general membership does, in fact, set the course of an organization; that, in fact, it represents that population it purports to represent.

One can prevent the organizer from "running" the organization by such devices as the careful selection and education of organizers. Further, a precise, generally accepted definition of the role of the organizer within the organization is also useful. And it is important that the employer of the organizer be outside the organization (as is often the case with baseball umpires and other specialists who need to be shielded from the internal politics of the organizations that they influence). Thus, the relationship of the organizer to the organization is created in such a way as to force the organizer to work toward creation of an effective democratic process that he does not dominate.*

Leaders and Followers

The term "leader," as used here, deliberately distinguishes between "leaders" and "those in charge." A person "in charge" of an organization need not have followers, although people in charge of democratic organizations always have followers.

Some facts about leadership follow from the above distinctions.

First, leadership is very difficult to perceive since it involves discerning how people would act if not subject to sanctions. A low-income person is more likely to get a job in an antipoverty program if he pretends to be a leader of low-income people. Similarly, many low-income people are more likely to be rewarded if they pretend that one or another political or other pro-

---

*Such an education-employment structure for organizers has not in the past been available. It is now being developed. For further information send inquiries to the Institute for Socio-Analysis, 4202 Angeles Vista Boulevard, Los Angeles, Calif., 90008.

minent figure is their leader. Thus, leaders and followers consensually validate pretenses which become the official (although not the actual) reality in groups, organizations, and communities. Since these pseudo-realities become institutionalized, the true state of leadership may only emerge during moments of crisis or rapid change. It may then become clear who would be followed in what ventures in the absence of subtle institutionalized coercion.

Second, although leadership may in part *result from* the extraordinary skills and abilities of some people, it does not *consist in* personal traits. It is developed and strengthened through an interaction process. For this reason leadership training programs for low-income people are usually useless. Without social structures and processes within which leadership can flourish, potential leaders lack arenas in which to exercise and improve their talents. On the other hand, power-oriented organizations of low-income people provide excellent arenas for leadership education.

Third, leadership is expressed in form as well as in content. The *forms* of leadership are commonly referred to as leadership styles. These might include the extent to which, and ways in which, a leader uses directive language; how or when he manipulates, conceals, repeats himself in his contacts with others as a leader; or how he attracts the attention of others when acting as a leader. Style would include the physical grace of a leader, his capacity to speak to people of differing backgrounds in their various ways. A leader with one style may spend much time quietly listening; one with another style may tend to talk much of the time. The style of a leader includes the "forms in thinking" through which he helps to define courses of action for himself and his followers.

The dynamics of leadership include both the style employed by leaders and the content or program areas in which their leadership is exercised. For example, one leader may be fiery, directive, and moralistic in style while choosing to exercise her leadership only in affecting the official educational process in which schoolchildren are involved.

The following brief account illustrates some of the dynamics of leadership by one woman in a power-oriented organization of low-income people.

Mrs. Black / *Stout, volatile, intelligent, and earthy, Mrs. Black is a Negro welfare recipient in her thirties who lives, husbandless, in public housing, with her several children. She has had little formal education, but is a widely respected leader in her neighborhood, a person with a sturdy sense of her own dignity and of that of her associates.*

I remember her ponderous grace as she walked into a meeting with a hearty "Good evening, ladies and gentlemen" and beamed at the friendly responses from both black and white colleagues. After some good-humored gossip about the week's events, she slowly settled onto an entirely inadequate chair. In that meeting, as in many others, her opinions were received with respect, but her recommendations were no more likely to be accepted than were the recommendations of several other leaders.

Although Mrs. Black has spent much time in quiet day-to-day organizational work, she has a special fame as a curmudgeon. A local politician or administrator, faced with an independent, critical delegation of people from a low-income neighborhood, usually tries to present himself as nice and friendly and honest, while at the same time resenting the presumption of uneducated people who question some aspect of his work. His instinct is to avoid a blunt discussion of issues raised by the delegation. It is to respond with an ingratiating (but evasive and calculating) politeness. The delegation members quickly sense that they are "getting the run-around." At such moments, Mrs. Black would begin to talk with a steadily increasing tempo and volume until wave after wave of angry rhetoric was cascading over her hapless opponent as she also advanced toward him. His reaction, commonly one of visible fright, would be merrily described in the neighborhood for weeks or months thereafter.

One of the projects of the neighborhood organization to which Mrs. Black belonged was to get a grocery store located in the vicinity. An urban renewal clearance project had forced the previously nearby stores and supermarkets to move and nothing had replaced them. The members of the organization felt that the urban renewal agency, responsible for the disappearance of the stores, should arrange for at least a small grocery store in the neighborhood, especially for the use of elderly people without available transportation. At one meeting, Mrs. Black urged her colleagues to action in approximately the following words: "My idea is to take all the mothers and all the babies and to push together to go down to that office and to stand and to wait until they get a store. . . . It does not make any sense for a few to do all the work. We have been going down there in sixes and sevens and all we get is talk, talk, talk. We are tired of talking, we want action. If you want something done, you got to do it yourself. We've sent around notices and knocked on doors asking people to come out and nobody did. Everybody had some sort of excuse. We had baby-sitters for you and cars to come right to the door. Door-to-door service. Still you have excuses. There is no reason for this. Now, what's your problem? Pure laziness, that's what it is. If you get off your behinds you can get something done. There is no reason for these excuses."

In response to this short lecture some members of the organization were embarrassed and some mumbled statements such as "She sure is right," or "Yes, that's right, I guess we are lazy." But no one volunteered to go down to the urban renewal office with their children. At the end of the meeting some of the informal conversations suggest reasons for this reluctance. There were comments like "What's the use of doing anything if the same people have to do it over and over again?" Some claimed they were too busy and others that they would not expose their children to all those various activities mentioned by Mrs. Black.

In some ways, the leadership of Mrs. Black resembles that of leaders everywhere; the use of repetition to drive home points, concrete illustrations of general themes, a careful sensitivity to opinions of her followers and associates, a tendency to define a collective course of action as involving a struggle between forces of good and evil, and to personalize events that may arise from social factors.

In other respects Mrs. Black's style is more likely to be found among low-income leaders than among the leaders of groups in more "comfortable" neighborhoods. There is, for her, a freedom of expression of anger and a blunt way of speaking to associates and opponents alike. She would often be considered rude and vulgar by audiences elsewhere in society. In fact, she gains part of her following through being able vividly to express attitudes and feelings that are generally felt in her neighborhood, but not generally so well expressed.

As a compelling, vivid, and sometimes an almost heroic figure in the dreams unfolding in her neighborhood, often the center of everyone's amused and/or amazed admiration, Mrs. Black can be said to have *more* leadership style (in relation to the content of what she says) than is often the case in more sedate neighborhoods. And in any classification of leadership styles, hers certainly resembles styles and tendencies toward styles very common in urban low-income neighborhoods in the United States.

On the other hand, some of Mrs. Black's limitations as a leader are reflected in her style of leadership. She tends to be pugnacious in her neighborhood, in meetings of her organization, as well as in confrontations, and this has made her many enemies. Sometimes she is angry in situations in which anger is not regarded as appropriate by her colleagues, and she may then be treated as a clown, a person to laugh tolerantly at, but not a person to follow. She holds her leadership position partly through her friendship with the president of her organization; it is not clear to what extent she would otherwise be followed. The president, a black woman with a more complex and flexible leadership style, has a much larger following than does Mrs. Black.

The Self-Help Leader as Specialist

Most low-income leaders today are specialists. One can articulate eloquently the anger and aspirations of people with little income, but cannot very well chair a meeting. Another may specialize in matters that deal with personal relationships, but avoid making public speeches. Generic leadership abilities, in contrast, require long-term socialization into a variety of tasks in complex organizations.

Thus, leaders in low-income populations find it difficult or repugnant to relate to genteel society on its terms, yet lack the skill and vision to develop enough power to force genteel society to relate to them on mutually acceptable terms. As a result, leaders tend to isolate themselves into small cliques that dispense with democracy and dwindle in size. This outcome stems, not from the personal traits or energy levels of low-income leaders; rather it derives primarily from the situation in which they find themselves in low-income populations. A competent organizer, relating primarily to the general membership of an organization, can prevent or reverse this trend to oligarchy and impotence. Enemies of an organization, aware of the functions of competent organizers, naturally seek to isolate an organizer from the leadership of the organization with which he is associated.

Structural Stresses

The other major problem in organization maintenance which we will consider has to do with the durability of the internal structure of power within such organizations.

When the internal structure of power of an organization collapses, the members may suddenly find their own situations undefined, or redefined in a fashion that no longer allows them to anticipate the future. Other definitions, organizations, and objects immediately appear different to them and may acquire more salience in their lives. The members lose the power that they have been able to exercise by virtue of their position in the organization and their relationship with other members within it. We may say that when an organization fails to develop and maintain its internal structure of power, the members find themselves in a *power bind* insofar as the organization is concerned.

We will not discuss here the many determinants of a power bind. It is enough to note that the disintegrative process set in motion by the onset of the power bind may be reversed at any stage. Or it may continue a downward spiral until all the formal and informal social structures that bolstered the organization have been pulverized and the former members remain completely alone, with no remaining bonds among them. For the members who are now alone, cut off from each other, there is apathy, anxiety, restlessness, floundering, heightened suggestibility, a tendency to believe in bizarre and unexpected events, and susceptibility to wild rumors and panic. Members may turn inward to create private paranoid interpretations of the situation as a last desperate and irrational effort to cope with the danger. Members now seek private security regardless of what happens to their former comrades. No longer is there any confidence in support from a nurturant surrounding group. Even long-established interpersonal relationships may be broken. Former reactions of childish helplessness in the face of overwhelming danger become reactivated. People so affected may begin to make dire predictions about what will happen next. There may be an increase in random behavior that is not goal directed. Minor events trigger severe anxiety as omens of further disasters. People find it difficult to concentrate and engage in neurotic or even psychotic behavior.

In practice the power bind does not often run the full course to complete privatization and demoralization. If the danger recedes, the fragments of the organization may be able to reconstruct it again. Even if the danger remains, the new collectivity may develop into a social movement that can regulate its members and exercise force enough to overcome the danger. If so, a new organization eventually crystallizes from the successful movement and may be less vulnerable to the stresses that caused the former collapse.

Organizations of low-income people tend to be exceptionally vulnerable to the power bind, and for obvious reasons. Most solutions involve adequate funding through the organization, a coalition with enough other organizations to enable the exercise of substantial power, and the presence of a competent organizer who understands the power bind process, who can keep calm and determined as he skillfully helps others to do likewise. Under those circumstances, the role of the organizer undergoes a considerable shift of emphasis. While attempting to reduce the negative impact of the power bind, he addresses himself to the population in which the organization is based; he helps that population to repair or rebuild an alternative reality and the decision-making process necessary for the effective exercise of power within that reality.

The Path to Power

Let us turn now to the final discussion of this report: the creation of power through the self-help reorganization of that majority of households within the United States with incomes of less than $10,000.

Typical self-help organizations of low-income people show many evidences of nonrational and undemocratic functioning. Their membership, however, does include a higher proportion of intelligent, energetic, practical, and idealistic people, even though there has not been available enough good organizational technology to enable such personal virtues to find effective collective expression.

Yet we have succeeded in helping low-income populations in several parts of the United States to create and maintain effective and democratic power-oriented organizations of the kind described previously. And we know, in general, how to select and educate competent organizers for such organizations.

If these low-income organizations can develop throughout the United States and coordinate themselves as a single social force, there can then be organized populations of slightly higher income for similar goals. These two subpopulations would then be able to mobilize a majority of the people in a variety of actions toward achieving social change. This organized majority would then seek to make coalitions on specific issues with organizations and collective interests in more affluent sectors of American society. The entire process would begin slowly, uncertainly gather momentum, and come to a steady state only after several decades of effort. However, this effort should begin to result in some social change long before a steady state is achieved. Our experience to date suggests that relationships among organizations should be strengthened by giving priority to developing communication among organizations and their members. The presence of competent organizers and a rapid expansion in communications will make unnecessary the hierarchies which have, in the past, been required to coordinate national efforts.

Up to the previous paragraph, what has been written has been solidly based in organizational practice over a long period of time. Future efforts, however, will depend heavily on assumptions about households that are neither affluent nor lowest-income in character. The major assumptions we make about this population are as follows:

1 | Other things being equal, this moderately deprived population has more of a stake in organization for social change than is the case in the affluent sectors of the American population.

2 | Moderately deprived people may come to believe in the necessity and urgency of societal democratization in inverse ratio to the amount of their income. Of course, the anger endemic in deprived populations can deflect from societal democratization unto assaults on competitors or rival groups. However, rational organizational structures and organizers can counter such irrational possibilities.

3 | Other things being equal, marginally employed young ghetto men and women will more easily believe that democratization requires substantial social change than is the case for those with stable higher incomes. Given the outlook of an organizer, it is easier to convince poor people than more affluent ones that major social change is needed.

4 | It is easier to convince moderately deprived people that democratization is desirable than to convince them that it is possible.

5 | Through the experience derived from participation in rational democratic organizations, moderately deprived people will attain a far higher "level of consciousness" than that achieved through trade unions, political parties, or other power-related groups. Given appropriate conditions for socialization, most moderately deprived people will acquire a complex stock of knowledge concerning social process and increased abilities to make social analyses.

6 | Ideas, and language in which to communicate ideas, are necessary and sufficient conditions for reorganization of the moderately deprived population. For example, no combination of conventional political organization and use of mass media is as effective as skillfully arranged face-to-face conversations in determining the actions of the moderately deprived. This is *not*

to say that rational democratization of the local organization can be easy, quick, uneventful, without setbacks, or unrelated to such problems as the tendency of democratic process to result in oligarchy.

7 | No substantial sector of American society, within or outside the moderately deprived population, has had much experience with democratic social processes or human* (as distinct from bureaucratic or personally autocratic) organizations.

8 | The people in the moderately deprived population will plunge spontaneously into an effort to democratize their society only under extraordinary conditions. Such a movement could arise during a time of national crisis in which the alternative of democratization is widely discussed as a live option. During most times people in the moderately deprived population begin gradually to work for democratization of the society by means of collective struggle (a) through democratic processes and (b) to resolve problems immediately apparent to them.

*For an extended discussion of this question, see the unpublished paper "Human Organization" (1970), written jointly by Lois Haggstrom and myself and available through the Institute of Socio-Analysis, 4202 Angeles Vista Boulevard, Los Angeles, Calif., 90008.

To know that you are not alone is a freeing
experience because it can give you hope.
—Pamela Allen

16

Consciousness-Raising: Self-Help in the Women's Movement

JANET NORMAN

What is "consciousness-raising"? Robin Morgan[1] has formulated its characteristics in the Women's Movement.

I | The "bitch session" cell group

  A | *Ongoing consciousness expansion*

    1 | Personal recognition and testimony

    2 | Personal testimony—methods of group practice

      a. Going around the room with key questions on key topics

      b. Speaking out experience at random

      c. Cross-examination

    3 | Relating and generalizing individual testimony

  B | *Classic forms of resisting consciousness—or how to avoid facing the awful truth*

  Including:

    Anti-womanism

    Glorification of the oppressor

    Excusing or feeling sorry for the oppressor

    Romantic fantasies

    "An adequate personal solution"

    Self-cultivation, rugged individualism

    Self-blame

    Ultra-militancy, etc.

  C | *"Starting to stop"—overcoming repressions and delusions*

    1 | Reasons for repressing one's own consciousness:

      a. Fear of feeling one's past wasted and meaningless;

      b. Fear of despair for the future, etc.

    2 | Analyzing which fears are valid and which invalid.

    3 | Discussing possible methods of struggle in a historical context, an individual context, and a group context. Daring to share one's experiences with the group.

    4 | Understanding and developing radical feminist theory. Using the above techniques to begin to understand our oppression. Analyzing whatever privileges we have, white skin, education, class, etc., and to see how these help perpetuate our oppression and that of others.

    5 | Consciousness-raiser (organizer) training, so that every woman in a given "bitch session" cell becomes an "organizer," in turn, of other groups.

II | **Consciousness-raising actions**

III | **Organizing**
   A | *Helping new people start groups*
   B | *Intra-group communication and actions*
   1. Monthly meetings
   2. Conferences

The CR group is widely used in the Women's Movement as a means of relating the individual differences in personality and outlook within small groups. It is a politicizing tool aimed at increasing awareness of social issues gained through the realization of the commonality of women's dilemmas. It is in some ways related to the encounter group but has differing aims. The original "T" groups were used as a socialization process or therapy, and the Human Potential Movement, the Esalen Institute, and other self-awareness centers may be seen as a revival of spirituality in the United States. However, these are all apolitical, whereas the CR group is not.

The size of the group varies. Many remain "open" for some months, but when a steady core of committed women emerges they may close the group to new persons, since as the growing together progresses it becomes harder for a new person to be included. Groups may be between five and fifteen—or larger.

It seems that most women join a CR group when "the shoe pinches" in some way or another in their own individual lives. They are seeking a new self-awareness. In the group they find a new acceptance and understanding and out of sharing develop new confidence and capabilities for expression and action. Many women find this makes changes in their lives. However, unlike members of a therapy group, from the beginning, the women do not see themselves as lacking, sick, or deviant, but rather seek to understand the way they are affected by society and to discover new ways to approaching dilemmas of living. New friendships and group support emerge. There are, of course, many obstacles and conflicts—how these are overcome or used seems to depend largely on the structure, if any, adopted by each group. As Pamela Allen writes of her group, Sudsofloppen,

We are a group which believes that there is always a structure, the issue is to consciously choose one that will encourage our growth rather than just hope that it will happen. We think this way because our early activity was consciously unstructured— we thought—and we found that letting things happen meant that the strongest personalities controlled the meetings and that it was very easy to avoid areas of discussion that were difficult.[2]

Usually a topic will be agreed upon by the group prior to the meeting. Then each woman will speak for a given time—not more than ten or fifteen minutes, uninterrupted, on the topic from her own personal experience, not theories. After each person has spoken, there is general discussion, and then each person makes some generalizations or summing up of the individual personal experiences, to widen the meaning of this for all women and their oppression in society. Meetings are sometimes limited in length.

The question of leadership arises in any small group. Some CR groups adopted ways of avoiding scapegoating or dominance by the more articulate. Some found that power struggles developed. Some relied on charismatic leaders—sometimes a very "honest" woman would promote opening up by others. Some groups were dependent on a leader to conduct the meeting. However, many groups adopted a system of rotating leadership to overcome problems of dominance by a few. There seems to be a need for some controlling or focusing of the discussion. If one person is responsible at each meeting for timing, keeping people to the topic, this may help prevent bad feelings and keep order. Some groups, however, felt no need for any leader.

A CR Group

About eight of us started a CR group, and after three months or so a core of seven emerged. (Some eleven people being involved at one time or another, but for various reasons—time of meeting, leaving the city, and so on—four dropped out.) We were all probably "middle-class," but from different backgrounds and living different life-styles. We met in a different home each week. Coming to the weekly Sunday evening meetings regularly was in itself an issue. Some found commitment to a group produced mixed feelings. There were practical difficulties—husbands, children, conflicting interests, and self-doubt. However, most felt the group played a very significant part in our lives. It was a place where people could be taken seriously, could feel free to express doubts, where efforts were made to avoid criticism or judgments.

None of us had known each other before we came to the group. We were very different. One, a nurse of twenty-four, had an interesting job, plenty of friends, male and female; a secretary, twenty-nine, had worked her way through various businesses; a lawyer, thirty-four, was recently divorced; one at library school with a child of four; one married with a child of eight, politically active in the past; a writer of forty earned her living as a secretary; a social worker, thirty. We tried to keep to a structure, but were not always successful. It seemed that structure was essential to help us avoid hard feelings and to prevent gossip or slanging matches. We found that when someone left or missed a meeting, we felt let down—even if the reason for absence was quite understandable. It took some weeks of getting to know each other to begin to have the courage to open up about the things closest to us and about our mixed feelings about the group or people in the group, which often led to constructive new understanding of ourselves and the others. I found that small aspects of every woman's life, which we learn to accept from the day we are born, came to have new meanings. Why should women not go places alone? Why did many of us feel a diffidence about our work? Why had we not taken ourselves seriously? Why did we blame ourselves for so much?

The topics we discussed were women and work, women's sexual needs, women and politics, motherhood, the basic differences between man and woman, children, violence and sexuality, and so forth. Also, we felt it necessary to talk about the group, why we came, what were our aims, our expectations—what it meant to each one of us. Sometimes we discovered how misguided our perceptions and jealousies of each other were. Some of us had mixed feelings about coming to the meetings, but all felt they played a very significant part in our lives. Some of our initial feeling involved a stigma about friendships among women, having been brought up to consider male-female relationships the way to a successful adulthood. Our perceptions of the men in our lives changed too. We gained more confidence in ourselves and grew less open to being walked over by exploiting males in our personal and work lives. This too brought new difficulties—we sometimes felt we were becoming anti-men and did not like this; also, we felt badly about our own part in "sexist" games, that we were using our femininity and betraying ourselves and other women. There were political differences in the group, but on the whole, none of us were ready to jump on any bandwagons and we kept our separate lives. We felt, however, the need for more action as a group. Some of us attended monthly coordinated meetings at the Women's Center. One person made a move in her office to hold a meeting to discuss work problems (which had not happened for ten years), another took on the job of organizing a seminar and felt more confident in asserting herself. We all felt a joy in sharing our ups and downs, a growing together that added a new dimension to our lives. We learned a lot from each other about different life-styles and backgrounds. We came to express our difficult feelings about being unmarried and a failure or being married and envying the single their freedom.

Structure and Process

As in all groups, it seems crucial to express in-group feelings and also to re-assess aims, expectations, and feelings about the group. In discussing this with representatives of other CR groups, it was clear that many groups broke up or settled for action, as they felt limited by CR. However, it seemed to me at that time that often the group itself and its significance was not broached as a topic and thus became a block; for example, each person was living up to an undefined and unshared group "norm." However, discovery of differences and opening up often leads to renewal, and even if the group decides to disband at least it would be good to know why.

Generalizations and relating personal experiences expressed in the group to the position of women in society is also important to the goals of CR. Otherwise the group may turn inward, may behave more like a therapy or encounter group or, sometimes, a gripe session or futile intellectual argument.

How to Fight

Within the CR group, conflicts arise and some of these may threaten the existence of the group. However, it seems the function of such a group is to provide a working opportunity for these to arise and be dealt with constructively so that a growing process evolves. Too often in contemporary life, fear and avoidance surround conflicts and differences and prevent growth. Aggression turns inward and becomes destructive. CR is an attempt to deal with this problem in the Women's Movement. Some CR groups seem more effective than others in creating what Pamela Allen has called "Free Space."

Often, strong feelings arise within the group from differences of age, sexuality, marital status, possession of children, or career. These feelings are very strong, based on years of socialization, and may often be suppressed consciously or unconsciously. If progress in understanding is to evolve, these must be expressed. So trust must develop between members. Pamela Allen describes how essential it is to develop trust from the start: "Trust is what gives us strength to be honest; trust in oneself and in one's sisters in the group. There are many roadblocks in our way, probably the most important being our fear of taking ourselves and each other seriously. . . . Our first commitment to one another is to attend meetings regularly. We come to meetings on time and call if we will be late. We try to inform the group ahead of time if we will miss a meeting. . . . And always, we try to be aware of the individual needs of our members, both by giving a space for talk and perspective and by helping concretely when we can. . . . No other trust can develop if we cannot even trust that our group is a reality." Then fear of breakup of the group or fear of nonacceptance in the group becomes another obstacle to open expression: ". . . Precisely because the group does become so meaningful to our lives as we start to separate ourselves from dependence on male values and institutions, it is a temptation to transfer our identities onto the group, to let our thinking be determined by group consensus rather than by doing it ourselves. . . ."[3]

And further, "we came to learn the hard way that one of the key characteristics of an oppressed people is self-hatred, and that our tendency to take out our frustrations on one another was a sign of oppression."[4] Feelings of low worth make for low tolerance of weakness and jealousy of strength in others.

CR has served different functions in different sections of the Women's Movement. Cellestine Ware describes the movement's political divisions very clearly. Radical feminists see dangers in CR of failing to relate the CR group to action and failure to become aware of the wider issues in the movement. The Redstockings, a group of mostly white educated women in New York, saw CR not as an end in itself, but as a means to information, identifying objective conditions of women's lives, and analyzing methods of struggle against oppression. However, it is criticized for wasting too much time on fruitless discussion. The "Feminists" would use CR as an organizing tool alone. Radical socialists on the other hand would reject CR as any kind of revolutionary activity—as middle-class, anti-Marxist, subjective.

However, it seems to me a very important part of any serious political movement today, in the light of history and of our knowledge of organizing, to use CR to deal with in-movement conflicts and further understanding of the needs and perceptions of different people. This helps avoid dogmatism or rigidity that promotes further repression. Aggression, the dynamic moving impulse in people, should not be rejected but turned to good purpose, toward growth and understanding. I saw an example of this in a group of about sixty women in another city. A discussion of woman-to-woman relationships in general turned onto the group itself and one woman, a "housewife," had the courage to stand up and let out a torrent of anger about the way she felt looked down upon by "intellectual" unmarried women. This led to an opening up of many women's feelings and to a new understanding on all sides.

It is unfortunate when CR becomes separated from action, but I think that the two are not alternatives. On the contrary, they are traveling the same road, one that has many twists and turns.

Women are getting together to search for new ways—to assess their needs, to try out new ways of living, and to develop new ways of growing and becoming involved in helping each other to grow. Perhaps many can say with Pamela Allen: "We have indeed grown . . . both in our love for one another and in our understanding of our society. We think the love has grown because we stopped looking self-consciously for it and began to struggle together instead. And our beginning to relate to our society has given a central unity to our lives. We are no longer drifting, relating passively to life; rather we are attempting through an intense relationship to society to affect history, to act instead."[5]

Part V

Communities
of the
Unwanted

17

Patients—75; Professionals—0: The Lodge Program in Community Rehabilitation

DAVID H. SANDERS

A research completed in 1961 and published in 1964 under the title *Social Psychology in Treating Mental Illness: An Experimental Approach*, edited by George W.

Fairweather, revealed that highly cohesive task groups of chronic mental patients could be formed. Such groups functioned relatively autonomously and demonstrated an ability to maintain their members and social organization. However, when released from the hospital individually they made only a slightly better community adjustment than a control group who had participated in a more traditional hospital treatment program.

Despite the success and considerable advantages of the small-group approach when contrasted with the more traditional treatment program, 16.67 percent of psychotics with more than two years' previous hospitalization never left the hospital during the initial year. Moreover, 35.42 percent of the chronics who left returned to the hospital within six months. Thus, 52.09 percent of this population was in the hospital at the end of the six-month follow-up period.

Further analyses of the data showed that patients who remained out of the hospital the longest were those who were employed and who also had a socially supportive living situation in the community. The most profound and significant result of this study was that posthospital adjustment is unrelated to hospital behavior *but* is highly related to the posthospital social situation in which the patient finds himself.

In light of these findings, it seemed necessary to move task groups into the community where they would be presented with the problems of maintaining themselves in a productive and supportive work-living situation. It was believed that the recidivism rate would be reduced, employment increased, and the patient's perception of himself would be enhanced.

A task group of patients was organized in the hospital and later moved into a community lodge as a unit after they had lived and worked together in the hospital for a few weeks. While in the hospital, this group was presented with problems that they would have to solve after arriving in the community. These problems involved creating a work-living organization, caring for each other, preparing and purchasing their own food, securing employment, keeping books, etc.

SOURCE: Reprinted with permission from *Attitude*, vol. 1, no. 7, (November/December 1970).

After moving into the community, a janitorial business was organized to provide employment for the lodge members. This was an excellent task since it allowed for a diversity of work such as administrative jobs, procedures for receiving and processing job orders, transporting members to and from jobs, and participating in work groups or crews depending upon an individual's qualifications, ability, and adjustment.

The goal of this research, then, was to provide a total community social subsystem for the rehabilitation of chronic psychotics and to contrast it with an existing hospital small-group treatment program on the reduction of the hospital recidivism rate, improvement in self-enhancement, and the reduction of continuous hospitalization. Both experimental groups had the same hospital treatment program. Matched patients participated in the two rehabilitation programs.

After the experimental group was moved to the community lodge, it took approximately one month to create an organization that met the living and working needs of the members. Subsequent to the establishment of the janitorial service and the purchase of supplies and equipment, jobs were secured through advertising. Gradually an administrative, legal, bookkeeping, work, and training organization was developed where specific roles were clearly delineated. For example, one member became the coordinator replacing the research staff member who had been responsible for the day-to-day operation of the work aspects of the lodge. He was responsible for securing jobs and estimating their cost, arranging transportation to and from work, chairing executive committee meetings, taking care of the administrative paper work, and running the necessary and numerous errands that arise in daily living.

Coordination of the lodge's activities progressed from professional to lay personnel. The first coordinator was a psychologist with several years' professional experience. The second coordinator was a graduate student. Improvement in social organization and member behavior progressed so well that an attempt was made to find out if individuals who were not professional persons could coordinate such a social system. Two lay persons with no formal education or experience in treating mental patients were hired and trained to supervise the lodge, replacing the research staff member. Morale at the lodge took a sharp upward turn. A noticeable increase in business occurred along with a marked improvement in the members' performance.

During the thirty-three months of the lodge operation, twenty of the seventy-five men who resided there became leaders of work crews; one member was the cook for the entire course of the lodge's existence. He was responsible for planning and preparing the meals as well as ordering all the food. Several members worked in the kitchen as assistant cooks or dishwashers. Another member was the business manager. He kept the books and telephoned for appointments with customers. Five men assisted the coordinator by either learning or relearning how to drive. They transported members to and from jobs and ran the many errands required on the job.

Although the great majority of the members remained workers in the work crews, some crew members became specialists in rug cleaning, stove cleaning, floor stripping, and different types of gardening. This specialization required motivation, incentive, and hard work. It resulted in the need for further refinement of the work organization. A differential salary schedule, annual leave, and sick leave were additional refinements developed.

Initially, all members received the same rate of pay. Later, the role they played, the amount of responsibility they had, the quantity and quality of work, and their initiative and motivation determined the amount of money they received. These salaries, incidentally, came from money that was sent to the janitorial service by its customers. Ninety percent of the total amount received weekly was paid to the members according to a differential pay schedule worked out by the members. Initially, 10 percent was held in reserve to be used to purchase supplies for the business. The research staff approved this savings because it appeared that such an amount would afford the members the opportunity to, at least in part, purchase their *own* supplies with their *own* money for their *own* business.

Organizational and problem-solving advice to the members of the lodge was the main obligation of consultants. One research staff member was the permanent lodge consultant and spent from four to six hours a week at the lodge for consultation and the completion of research forms. A local physician saw members for their medical problems in his downtown office. Parenthetically, when a member demonstrated irresponsibility, inability, or unwillingness to take his medication, the peer-nurse, a lodge member himself, was designated to make certain that he took his prescribed dosage at the proper time. A Stanford University auditor was a continuing consultant on bookkeeping procedures and consultation was also secured from the university commissary about the purchase and preparation of food.

All roles in the lodge—members, research staff, consultants—were clearly defined for each individual and well known to the members. These ex-mental patients operated their own business. They had their own trucks, power equipment, and other tools; and the lodge served as a residence for them as well as a base of operation for their daily work. Satisfactory and adequate work performance was attained and repeat work was common. After the janitorial service had been established, a gardening service was organized; general hauling and painting was also done.

New problems arose as time passed. Procedures were recognized by the members: A program for the orientation of new members to the lodge and community living was established; a work training program for new members was begun. A two-week trial period was established for new members during which their role behaviors were clearly defined. This trial period was initiated by the members because they soon learned if a new man was to remain at the lodge he had to contribute to its productivity. An executive committee was established as the policy-making and governing body of the lodge, and it convened when needed. For some time it was comprised of all the crew chiefs, the cook, and the business manager. It ranged in size from five to ten men and was representative of the entire lodge population for the greater part of the first two years of the lodge's existence. During this time, the committee made decisions about work and living procedures and it made decisions about behavioral deviations.

However, despite its appropriate decision-making, it became less and less representative of the entire membership because it was comprised only of the leaders. As a consequence there was a rebellion among the workers and they petitioned the executive committee to allow them representation. The committee rejected the workers' proposal.

The research staff had the power to veto any committee decision considered to be detrimental to the lodge as a whole, but it rarely used the veto. On this occasion, however, the staff vetoed the committee's decision. The committee was then reorganized so that all members could attend any committee meeting of their choice. All members, leaders and workers, had one vote. Thus, everyone's view was finally represented and morale again improved.

This example demonstrates what had historically been a divergent point of view about the purpose of the lodge between the research staff and the members of the executive committee. The staff had always held the view that the lodge existed for two reasons, each of equal importance; namely, for the rehabilitation of the members as well as for their employment. Thus, the staff was more tolerant of behavior that would be considered abnormal or deviant. However, the leaders had increasingly stressed and established the norm that work was the single most important aspect of the lodge and they were, therefore, less tolerant of any deviant behavior that might question the importance of work.

This split usually remained implicit but occasionally became an open point of contention. It eventually led to a revolt of the workers and one of the few staff vetoes. Only in cases where a member was asked to leave because of his nonproductiveness as a worker had the veto been used.

Decisions by the executive committee regarding the expulsion of members who broke societal norms and whose behavior could, in turn, bring societal authorities in conflict with the lodge were wholeheartedly supported by the staff. It is noteworthy here that the work-rehabilitation conflict was intensified when the two lay leaders were hired. This occurred because they initially supported the work norm rather than the rehabilitation norm.

The autonomy of the lodge members increased steadily. This was not only shown by a progression from professional to lay leaders, but also by the increased responsibility that the members took for their own behavior. No professional person or research staff member resided at the lodge, but a staff member was on consultation call twenty-four hours a day. Members of the lodge designated one of the members to be responsible for the lodge. He made decisions when problems arose. He had separate sleeping quarters where a telephone was available. It is interesting to note that some members were considered by other members to be incapable of performing these duties. To help such individuals become qualified, a training program was established. At the completion of the training program, the executive committee determined whether an individual was capable of assuming this responsible position or if he had to continue his training.

The total sample for the study was 333—183 were in the non-volunteer-nonlodge group; the remainder consisted of 150 matched patients, with 75 in the volunteer-lodge group and 75 in the volunteer-nonlodge group. Compared to their matched control, a significantly greater proportion of the individuals in the lodge situation were able to remain out of the hospital and to assume employment. As far as time in the community is concerned, 65 percent of the lodge group remained out of the hospital for the first six months compared with 24 percent of the control. Thirty-five percent of the control never left the hospital, while, of course, all of the lodge group had.

In regard to employment, 50 percent of the lodge group were employed full time for a six-month follow-up period, while 79 percent of the matched control group were totally unemployed. Only 3 percent worked for the full six months. Furthermore, these results obtained for the next three and one-half years of follow-up. And the cost for lodge members was $6.37 per day compared to $14.34 in the hospital. When the lodge members used some of their earnings to defray expenses, the cost was reduced to $3.90 per day.

The success of this experiment clearly shows that chronic mental patients are in need of a subsociety which will sustain them in the community in a constructive and productive life. The treatment modalities that now exist are just the opposite. Even if the chronic can leave the hospital, which is difficult enough, he has further difficulty obtaining employment and then holding it, and many do not remain in the community for any significant length of time. When they do, they often remain socially isolated, stay in their rooms watching TV, and have little social life.

At the lodge, there was continuous social stimulation, employment, and companionship. These men built for themselves a sub-community with its own norms. They depended upon one another for support, something they could not have done independently. Furthermore, it was a style of life that was entirely acceptable to them and to their neighbors. As far as the larger community was concerned, these ex-mental patients were continuously moving away from the stigma of mental illness. The community viewed the lodge as a residence and a business where responsible men lived and worked at something constructive. They contributed financially to the community. And they accepted the community's norms.

As far as work was concerned, this group of men completed more than 3,000 jobs in two and three-quarter years and they worked almost continuously after the lodge was opened. As a group, they earned more than $52,000 during this period.

The possibility of such a subcommunity becoming eventually self-sustaining was also subjected to test. The opportunity to explore this occurred because local, state, and federal agencies did not utilize the results of this successful research project in establishing it as a new service program. Because of this, the lodge members agreed to assume full responsibility themselves. They did so successfully. By the termination of the study, operation of the lodge was completely autonomous. The road to autonomy was not completely problem-free; indeed, the lodge members have encountered many problems and faced severe crises. Nevertheless, the group has remained in the community, operating and supporting a total living-working situation by themselves.

But all of the above-mentioned statistics fail to reveal the perceptions of the individual member gained upon interview. For in these structured interviews, the common denominator of feeling was the enjoyment of the freedom that accompanies a productive self-sustaining community role.

The research regarding this unique community subsystem is discussed in detail in a book published in September 1969, which is titled *Community Life for the Mentally Ill: An Alternative to Institutional Care* by Fairweather, Sanders, Maynard, and Cressler.

Observations and voluminous data collected during the course of the three years the community lodge program was in operation have led to the conclusion that certain operating principles for community programs involving chronic mental patients are essential if such programs are to restore such individuals to a participating role in our society.

The participants must have a stake in the community lodge. *Throughout the course of the lodge experiment, it was obvious from repeated interviews with members, their neighbors, and customers, that the lodge members were proud of their organization. They wanted it to succeed. The members often remarked that the janitorial and gardening service was their business. The feeling of identification with the success of the business was clearly enhanced by ownership of it. This appears exceedingly important when the norms of our culture are taken into account. Great value is placed upon the ownership of property—particularly the means of production. With individuals who have not achieved prestige in this society, the personal values attached to the ownership of property is very great indeed. When an organization managed and controlled by mentally ill individuals is a success, the feelings of accomplishment are intense.*

Any community lodge designed for chronic mental patients must give as much autonomy to its members as is possible, *consistent with their behavioral performance. Autonomy of action contributes to the members' stake in the organization, but it is such an important procedure that it is treated here as a separate and independent principle. When the participants in any social system, such as the lodge, are not initially capable of assuming full autonomy, the organization must necessarily be structured by outsiders who can establish the social system so that it has an opportunity to succeed in the broader society. However, the leadership roles of outsiders should be relinquished as soon as possible and here it is of the utmost importance that the test for degree of autonomy the members are capable of is based upon empirical fact rather than on the opinions of the helping professions. Such professional persons often perceive chronic mental patients as being far less capable than they actually are.*

The community lodge should have a vertical organization *so that a division of labor is possible and a meaningful role can be established for all members. One of the important characteristics of the lodge was that its vertical organization permitted upward mobility within the social system for those who were motivated and capable of assuming higher statuses. At the same time, however, a meaningful social position was established for any member who was not capable of assuming a higher status or did not aspire to such a social position. Thus it was possible for each member to find a job commensurate with his abilities and interests so that he perceived himself and was perceived by others as a contributing individual.*

Any community lodge must be compatible with its environment. *Its internal social organization and its physical location must be compatible with the broader society. The entire social organization of the created social system must be as close a facsimile to the larger environment as possible, consistent with the capacity of its participants. This is necessary because chronic mental patients who participate in such a community lodge will eventually wish to leave it and enter the larger society. Life in the community lodge, therefore, should stress those behaviors that will permit any resident of the lodge to make this transition without undue stress. Such elements as adequate rewards for performance and real-life tasks can be used as common elements in both the community lodge and the larger society.*

Community lodges designed for chronic mental patients must establish internal norms that are tolerant of deviant behavior that might be considered normative for that particular population. *Often, mentally ill persons have behaviors which it is very difficult for them to totally abandon. It is difficult, if not impossible, for many of these individuals to discard aberrant behaviors immediately upon entry into a community lodge. The members of the social system must be tolerant of these behaviors. In the lodge, for example, members were often hallucinating while talking with other members within the confines of the lodge itself. But after considerable training and effort, most of them were able to reduce such behavior on their jobs in the larger community. There was, for example, one member who openly hallucinated at the lodge and en route to the job. Upon arrival at the work site, he was informed by his member supervisor that no talking was permitted on the job. Usually, he was silent during the work hours. Upon reentry into the truck for the trip home, he began hallucinating—an acceptable behavior to his peers.*

Mobile entry and exit from the community lodge should be possible without penalty to the individual. *If the community lodge is voluntary, there will be continuous entry and exit from it. Free access to the larger community should be provided for residents in the lodge. A social atmosphere conducive to venturing further into the larger community without attaching penalties for such a move should be provided. This is important not only because many members will eventually leave the lodge, but also because leaders of the lodge will often hesitate to leave the group because they feel an obligation to it. The social norms of the community lodge, therefore, should encourage such departures.*

Individuals should perform as groups wherever possible. *From the last several years of experimentation, it seems exceedingly important that chronic mental patients have membership in a reference group. The norms of such groups set performance standards for the members, but even more important they provide a "home" for such individuals. It was a common practice in the lodge for members to return to it when they had failed in the larger community, and it is significant that many of these individuals did not return to the hospital.*

New community lodges should not be dependent for their existence upon the good will of the larger community in which they are implanted. *While it is important that community lodges are compatible with their environments, it is also important that they should be financed and supported by agencies that are not directly dependent upon the immediate neighborhood for total financial support. Chronic mental patients who reside in the community need time to become self-sufficient and they also need protection against the community pressures that might destroy their tenuous adjustment. The lodge did not become self-sufficient until its fourth year of operation. The members were sustained through the formative stages, when great insecurity prevailed, by the university, the nonprofit corporation, and moneys from the National Institute of Mental Health. These organizations supported the fledgling society at a time when it easily could have been destroyed.*

There are many other principles that one might present, but these would seem applicable to almost all community lodges that might be devised for the chronic mental patient.

18

Camphill Villages

SARAH BLACK

Introduction

One of the lesser-known but most interesting and enduring of present-day communes are the communities of the Camphill schools and villages for handicapped children and adults. The Camphill Movement was founded by Dr. Karl König (1902–1966) in Scotland in 1939, based on the teachings of Rudolf Steiner.

The movement has grown and now extends to England, Ireland, Holland, Germany, Switzerland, South Africa, and the United States.

Since my encounter with Camphill in Aberdeen in 1968, the interest, inspiration, some special freedom of thoughts and feelings, or some "insight" is always with me from that living example of community. In the third of the following selections, "A Breath of Camphill," I have tried to explain something of my glimpse of a whole new world of possibilities, a world perhaps that Steiner could actually "see."

The first two selections, written by Dr. König and reprinted from *The Cresset*, the journal of the Camphill Movement, include "The History of the Camphill Movement," which was written at its very beginnings and gives an idea of the very early days, and an excerpt from "Meditations on the Camphill Movement," which was written in 1959.

A. The History of the Camphill Movement
KARL KÖNIG

During the years of 1936 and 1937, a few young men and women gathered around a country doctor who had come to Vienna, the town of his birth, to build up a medical practice in one of the suburbs of that city. The doctor and his wife had been forced to leave Germany where he had worked for some time under the conditions Nazism imposed.

Under this doctor's guidance, the group of young people began to study anthroposophy and many an evening was spent in reading and studying and discussing Rudolf Steiner's work. The group consisted of young teachers, medical students, and a few artists. All of them had one thing in mind and that was not only to

SOURCE: Reprinted with permission from *The Cresset*, vol. XV, no. 3 (Summer 1969).

understand anthroposophy and to listen to the teachings of Rudolf Steiner, but to basically change their attitude to life.

They felt more or less clearly that Nazism was a sign that destructive forces in the world were coming to a peak and that something would have to be done to counteract this evil force.

But they knew that counteraction by means of force or mass movement would not be effective. They felt rather that a new understanding of the human being and of all nature and a devotional attitude to life in all its manifestations through living Christianity would be the necessary counterbalance to Nazism.

Through Rudolph Steiner's teaching they learned that thoughts and ideals alone would change nothing, but a change of attitude to life could do very much.

They decided to start a community outside a town, working the soil, educating children, and educating themselves through daily work, daily study, and daily devotion.

Then Nazism flooded Austria as well and these young people had to leave the country with the hope of finding one another again in some other country still free from oppression and racialism, which would be helpful in allowing people to live their lives as they think best. Each of these young men and women went through many adventures and setbacks. They had fled to Italy, Switzerland, France, Yugoslavia, Slovakia, Holland, and Britain. They often had no contact with one another and experienced much hardship and loneliness, until finally they all came to Britain where they decided to ask the authorities to agree to their ideas of starting a community and to give assistance.

Through chance and destiny, some helpful members of the Church of Scotland became interested and other friends in the northeast of Scotland offered a house on their own estate to the little group of refugees.

This house was an abandoned manse standing on a hill and overlooking a wide valley north of Aberdeen. It was the first actual roof over the heads of this small group. The estate owners provided them with potatoes, milk, and oatmeal. The doctor had been able to bring his furniture over from Austria, and after a few weeks the manse was ready for occupation.

The garden was dug, the walls painted, the debris and dust

cleared from the outhouses, and after two months, the first handicapped children arrived and the fees paid for them privately made it possible to begin to live a regular life. The good and strong ideals and the will to stick to them on the part of these few people overcame all difficult circumstances and this was encouraging and grand to see.

The 12th of May 1940 was a fateful day for the community, because, on this Whitsunday, all the male members were interned and ultimately sent to the Isle of Man. The women were left alone, and to begin with, they were uncertain as to whether to carry on what was begun or wait until the men returned. But they decided to carry on, and not only that; they decided to extend the work.

Just before the internment of the men took place, the community had many inquiries for places for children. The manse was too small to envisage taking any more children and so the community tried to find a better and a bigger place. Owing to the unforgettable kindness of a friend and father of one of the boys who was due to join us, Camphill estate was purchased and ready to receive us. Everything for the move to Camphill had been prepared and the date fixed when the men were interned and the move seemed for a moment impossible.

But the women were full of confidence and strength and faith. They moved to the new place on the 1st of June 1940, furnished the house, worked the gardens and fields, took care of the children and struggled through the early months until, in October, the first two men came back from internment camp, finding everything in the best of order.

From now on, the work gradually enlarged. The community now has a big house, a cottage and lodge, and twenty-two acres of ground. Throughout the winter, we had our own potatoes and a lot of fruit and vegetables. We have ten children and some more to come. Most of the men have returned from internment and the work is running according to our aims. We shall soon have some goats and pigs and already have hens. We hope to acquire a cow in the near future.

So again, faith and confidence guided the community through hard and bitter times to a better standard.

Our Future Aims

What we have established up till now has been described. But what are our further aims?

The true aims are to become a real community connected with the work on the land and in the house connected with our own children and those who have been given into our care.

Handicapped children are mostly outcasts of human society. They are children who are unable to speak or unable to work. Children who are unable to find a place in their own homes, who cannot find schools and training.

We want to try to share our work with them, to show them how to hold a spade and to dig, how to make a compost heap and how to plant vegetables. But we also want to show them how to learn about and to understand the world, to teach them to appreciate the beauty of the world and the kindness of men. We want to try to teach them to understand numbers, music, to help them to read and write, to teach them to paint and model and carve.

We shall have common meals, common joys, and common sorrows. We shall have the Sunday services with our children. And our children will begin to establish themselves in the community and find their own identities, because their environment is one of love and understanding.

We hope to receive more and more handicapped children. We hope in time to build a few more small houses for them and to establish a tiny village in which there is a community of outcasts who are not outcasts but active citizens who will make their own contribution, and who have faith in what is spiritual and love for one another.

These are our aims.

But there may be a question in the mind of the reader: Why do we want to make all this effort on behalf of handicapped children? Is it worthwhile, when there are perhaps more important tasks in these troubled times?

B. Meditations on the Camphill Movement

KARL KÖNIG

From the beginning, we had set ourselves the task of Curative Education. Some of us were trained in this work and the rest were willing to learn. We felt it as a kind of mission to devote ourselves to this work. Rudolf Steiner had given a new understanding of the handicapped child, and we had seen several homes and schools on the Continent and in Britain which were run on his lines, and we wanted to add yet another to the number. This was our first aim.

At the same time, we dimly felt what later became quite clear—that handicapped children were in a sense in a similar position as we ourselves. They were refugees from a society that did not want them as part of the community. We were political, these children were social, refugees.

The symbiosis between the children and ourselves seemed to work very well. Already the first children given into our care felt at home and we accepted them wholeheartedly into our midst. They gave to us the work we wanted to do. They provided us with the conviction that we were performing a necessary task and were not superfluous and useless people. Through them, we were enabled to earn our livelihood and no longer needed to be dependent on public welfare and charity.

The most important thing, however, was that our handicapped children demanded of us a particular way of life. It was not only that *we* were to train and educate them; through the simple fact of their special existence they demanded a set of qualities we had to develop.

They set us the task of developing patience, equanimity, and compassion. They asked for a new understanding of their peculiar modes of behavior. Each day we faced a new trial in humanity and self-education. A tremendous opportunity was given into our hands.

At the same time we had to learn to look after the grounds and gardens, the house, the cooking, and all the other domestic work as we had, from the beginning, decided not to employ others to do it for us. We made use of domestic and practical work as a means of educating and training the children who took part in it as far as they were able.

Our own children were part of the house-community and the

SOURCE: Reprinted with permission from *The Cresset*, vol. XV, no. 3 (Summer 1969).

supposed barriers between mentally defective and "normal" children were abolished. It was a revelation to see how "normal" the handicapped children can be in such circumstances. We realized their need to be accepted in a closed community that, on the one hand, provided shelter and, on the other, the right atmosphere in which they could unfold their potentials.

We gradually grew aware of the necessity and urgent claim upon us to undergo training in self-knowledge and self-recognition. Rudolf Steiner's teaching provided the directives we needed.

We also discovered that for the children as well as for ourselves religious forms of life were a necessity. The Sunday, the Christian festivals, the morning and evening prayers spoken in common became indispensable social factors. We observed how an ordered day gave our children security and how it helped us in our efforts to become our own masters.

In this way a closely knit fabric of human relations developed and became the basic structure of all our further attempts. The symbiosis between handicapped children and political refugees began to show results. Our peculiar situation combined with Rudolf Steiner's teaching gave us the possibility of growing into a new social order.

This tiny developing social order was the dough, the European destiny of ourselves the yeast, and thus the substance of the future Camphill Movement was provided.

C.   A Breath of Camphill
SARAH BLACK

> The welfare of a group of people who work together is the better, the less each single person claims the profits of his labors for himself. This means that the more he offers these proceeds to his fellows and the more his own needs are covered by the proceeds of the labors of the others and not by his own work, the better. . . . All social establishments in a community which contradict this law are bound to lead, after some time, to want and poverty.
>
> —Rudolf Steiner

I got off the bus a few miles from Aberdeen in an open fielded stretch of road. I found myself at the foot of a long wooded driveway. At the gate a man was working in the garden of the old lodge cottage. He saw me and stopped in his work to take my suitcase and to direct me to life in the Camphill community.

It *was* like entering another life, another time. It might have been in some middle European village—the broken English of this man's greeting, of the short oh-so-simple letter of welcome in my pocket, the German names—I felt the excitement, anticipation of a traveler in a foreign country. I was apprehensive. I was afraid of *handicapped children, spastics, mongols, the deaf, the blind,* and so on. I felt unqualified to cope with stifling labors of dedication and self-sacrifice. On the other hand I had felt irresistibly drawn by the children I had met on a brief visit and by the ideas and descriptions of the people who lived and worked in the community. I was curious about life in such a community and I was reminded too of the children I still missed whom I had looked after in a "home" in Switzerland.

From the moment I entered Murtle House I forgot about "handicapped children." I found a great welcome and an acceptance I had never felt before. No need to produce paper or plastic qualifications. I sat down to lunch with Anthony and Marcus and David and Kay and Janice. They began to tell me about Murtle. To be sure they were all very different. Some could not speak, some were very short or awkward at walking, one could not see, one had a big head, some would not talk to anybody, some came and hugged you. It was hard to guess at ages. But above all each child was very much of a person with a life to be lived. There were no "patients," no "nurses" (although one or two of the co-workers had had nurses' training), even the teachers were people. Everyone was called by first names. Each had a unique identity.

Living was as a big family. We all ate together and helped about the house. No one was paid wages; if anyone needed clothes or anything, money was provided. There were some thirty children in Murtle at the time; they slept in dormitories, not more than about five or six in a room. Some of the rooms were a lovely irregular shape; there were handmade wooden beds and windows looking out to the hills and down to the River Dee.

There were about eight co-workers who had little rooms near the children's.

First thing in the morning after getting washed and dressed there were prayers, a time we would all come together and perhaps sing a song; then we all went into the dining room for breakfast. It seemed to me a very good beginning to the day, that quiet moment together, like a sort of recognition of each other and our hope to understand each other better.

For the older children there was school. Classes were arranged according to age, despite enormous differences in intellectual development. But of course there were all kinds of differences. I went to see a geography class and I learned my own lesson! There was a girl in the class who delighted in pulling hair, and I discovered that she was an expert at it since mine was long and a good target. Intent on being wicked she started a fight with a boy. I went to separate them, but the teacher stopped me, in time for us to see a beautiful settlement between the two, who "made it up" and kissed each other.

There were various special sessions for individual children or those with common difficulties. There were all sorts of classes—singing, drama, eurythmy, painting, woodwork, and so forth. There were walks to see the piglets and walks through the trees, and the vegetable garden, which was worked by some older boys living in the garden cottage, to the bakery or the pottery at Newton Dee. There was always plenty of work for the older children who were able to help in the garden around the house and in the extensive grounds.

There were several layers of community: the children in the dormitory with whom I lived, all the people in Murtle House, then those in the other cottages on Murtle estate, and still others on the other two estates and from the Newton Dee Village*—all gathered together in the hall at Murtle to celebrate the seasonal festivals. There were perhaps two hundred children living in about fifteen houses on three estates.

*The Village is one of several where some of the young men and women go to live when they leave the schools. The Camphill Village Trust was founded in 1954, following Dr. König's meetings with parents, and the first Camphill Village started in Botton in Yorkshire in 1955.

As well as the geographic layers, there were layers in time and commitment too. There was a core of permanent "staff" people, some of whom had been there from the beginning; there were people studying Curative Education[1] for three years or perhaps they would stay only a year or two; there were transitory people intending to stay for shorter periods, and there were visitors. Among the co-workers were houseparents, teachers, therapists, artists, doctor, musicians, gardeners, and people who used whatever skills they had.

At the heart of the community were the children.

By the standards of the society outside, the children were severely handicapped physically and/or "mentally," and had often been considered ineducable. Their appearance or behavior would be considered quite bizarre. But at Camphill one felt that the stigma wasn't there—not that the handicap was denied but, rather, that it was accepted as fact. The children were just people, each one different. It was fascinating to learn from each his or her own way of communicating, and to realize that the nature and effect of any person's handicap is by no means obvious and that this cannot so easily be distinguished from the stigma, that is, the values and attitudes that a materialistic society attaches to it. While at Camphill I don't remember thinking at all about "handicapped children," that is, the kind of thinking involved in my apprehensions before going there and that abounds everywhere outside Camphill.

Another remarkable thing was the way the children, each with very different difficulties, could actually help each other and in so doing discover value in themselves. There was one severely paralyzed, totally palsied girl of seventeen. She was very frail; she could use only her eyes. It was thought that special arrangements would have to be made for her on what was to be a short stay at Murtle. However, she made it known that she did not want to be fed alone but wanted to be with everyone else in the dining room. What a surprise it was, too, to see that her special friends were the rough, difficult boys. One very maladjusted, disturbed boy of sixteen learned to carry her, feed her, and take her for walks in her wheelchair, although he was shy about doing so and often blushed. Describing their relationship in an article in *The Cresset*, the housemother wrote, "But what really wove between the two is difficult to speak about; it was a tender and mysterious bond between themselves, which we could only regard with great respect. . . . She is still with us at Murtle. Her contribution is a unique one and far outweighs the physical care she requires of others. It is a privilege to live with her and she herself has much to teach us."[2] Sometimes very extrovert, warm, or talkative children would help bring out a withdrawn one. Most interesting things happened every day among these unusual children.

The lovely northern skies, the hills, trees, fields, the river down below. Strange, gentle, odd-shaped architecture, carved wooden beds, candles, music, simplicity, peace.

It was hard work and often must have drained people of their energies. But somehow the community kept very much alive. People there a long time told me that it was the children that showed the way, from them the community learned how to live together in some kind of harmony.

Some Thoughts on Community

The life spirit in us seeks to break out. The fears that surround us all, the "media" that deafen and blind us, the parent and authority figures that dictate to our conscious self, make us cautious. Yet we strive to find an acceptance—often we get by from hour to hour, day to day, by cushioning ourselves with OKs, with a "normal" or acceptable outer makeup, a face with which to confront the world. But we need more than this and we find others to share those nagging feelings. However, so often those people, or those people of good or outwardly commendable appearance or status whom we seek to protect us or build up our makeup, we also despise or fear. So we limit ourselves, we constrict ourselves, we split up our lives, compartment ourselves.

For me, staying awhile at Camphill raised new questions, dispelled some fears, above all raised new hope, opened new doors. The children were all so different, unable to hide behind façades, or unwilling. One felt at once a new light, a new hope, for one's own spirit was allowed new space, yet too one saw one's own façades more clearly and could no longer depend so much on them. So it was both a freeing community and a demanding one.

The essence of the community was learning to understand and

live with these special children, but it was also learning *from* them how to live. Central to this and of crucial importance were the daily prayers, Sunday services, and the seasonal festivals—this was for me the outward expression of an acceptance of and a respect for everyone in the community and of sharing and hope. At these times it seemed to show so vividly that "community" is greater than the sum of its members. I remember, I think it was on Maundy Thursday, a "silent supper." Remarkably silent it was, for there were plenty of children who at all other times found it impossible to be quiet, or to respond at all to any social demands, or who were deaf and, of course, could not "hear" the silence.

> *In a community of persons working together, the well-being of the community will be the greater, the less the individual claims for himself the proceeds of the work he does; i.e., the more these proceeds he makes over to his fellow workers, and the more his own requirements are satisfied, not out of his own work, but out of work done by others.* [3]

Steiner discusses this "law" in his essay, emphasizing it not as an ideal but as an actuality. But how to achieve it? He says the only way out of egoism is through working for others, but "if any man works for another he must find in this other man the reason for his work; and if any man works for the community he must perceive and feel the meaning and value of this community, and what it is as a living, organic whole. He can only do this when the community is something other and quite different from a more or less indefinite totality of individual men. It must be informed by an actual spirit in which each single person has his part." Steiner talks of "spiritual mission," that each member of the "communal body" must have the *will* to contribute toward its fulfillment. ". . . The problem of the present day is how to introduce people into conditions under which each will, of his own inner, private impulse, do the work of the community. . . . No one, therefore, need try to discover a solution of the social question that shall hold good for all time, but simply to find the right form for his social thoughts and actions, in view of the immediate needs of the times in which he is now living."

Steiner says that the necessary "spiritual world conception"

will mean disillusionment for those wishing to be popular bene-
factors. He emphasizes that where the "law" operates it will be
of value on no matter how small a scale—it is not easy and "may
only be composed of a collection of tiny part-results."

So I felt very drawn to Camphill and spent a little time there
living and working with the children. I found others from all over
the world, some who with me felt a sense of being offered a new
way of living, more meaningful than any we had experienced
before, where the door seemed opened to the full possibilities of
being human, uncluttered by the rigid role structures and patterns
of our city mass-produced way of life. We found our anxieties
and conflicts, our despairs at the world we were born into, confronted and in a new way taken seriously. Yet some of us felt
unable to make a full commitment ourselves to this community
and felt our own lives or destinies were not there. Still, the time
we spent at Camphill was significant for us and would change our
lives wherever we might go. If this will of mine did not center on
this particular community, perhaps I would now search and find
my own.

Part VI

Self-Help in
Other Countries

19

European and North American Self-Help Movements: Some Contrasts

GUSTAVE A.
DE COCQ

In the last several decades the leading countries of Western Europe—the Netherlands, the Federal Republic of Germany, Denmark, and Great Britain, among them—

have all experienced tremendous changes, starting with the economic crisis of the thirties and followed by World War II and its massive consequences. In each of these countries the pressure of events necessitated the creation of far more enlightened and far-reaching social policies than had existed previously.

The degree to which social *policy* has been translated into social *services,* as well as the kind and extent of professionalism in social practice, varies in each country. Yet there can be no doubt that the concept of *social welfare,* as a guarantee of well-being for all citizens, is much more firmly established in these Western European societies than in North America. For diverse reasons—including the initial processes of immigration and the Protestant ethic that emphasizes the individual's responsibility for achievement through his own efforts—the state in North America has been seen as essentially antithetical, or at best neutral, in the individual's striving to achieve "the good life."

Conversely, in Western Europe the reciprocal relationship between individual potential and the social structure has been more widely recognized. Not only in the four countries mentioned, but also in others, acceptance of such a philosophy leads to a broader view of social responsibility and is reflected in all social institutions.

Thus we find sweeping, comprehensive, and generally accepted social services in the countries of Western Europe in contrast to those of North America. The climate of opinion in the United States and Canada is geared to the acceptance and provision of social services where there has been a clear breakdown of social functioning according to preconceived norms; to intervene in those cases where the individual, as a result of misfortune or accident, is not capable of reaching his potential by his own efforts. *In contrast, Western European programs generally address themselves to the population as a whole, rather than to specific individuals or groups who may have suffered a breakdown in social functioning.* Western European societies accept the responsibility to provide opportunities for the individual to develop his potentials, rather than reluctantly picking up the pieces when all other efforts have failed.

In spite of widespread social changes in the 1960's the countries of North America still view the individual as responsible for his own destiny and development. It is true that the social welfare measures in North America had their roots in Great Britain, in a penal code that protected the property rights of the non-poor, was severe in its punishment, and was rarely tempered by mercy. Thus, social service programs in the United States and Canada are often punitive in nature, e.g.: restrictive residence laws; emphasis on retribution in correctional and penal institutions; the belief that the unmarried mother should relinquish her child; cutting of allowances to unmarried mothers who have a second or third "illegitimate" child; close scrutiny of public assistance recipients; the encirclement of minority groups either on rural reservations or in urban ghettos.

Drawing this contrast does not imply that there are no restrictions on social welfare services in Europe, or that in North America there is no support for the reform and liberalization of welfare programs. But it seems clear that the climate of opinion in Western Europe encourages the development of comprehensive services, which aim to support the potential of people in general, rather than at salvaging particular groups of the underprivileged or unfortunate.

"Normal" vs. "Deviant" Functioning

In the prevailing North American view, social welfare, like health, is dichotomized; "normal" social functioning becomes a cutoff point *below* which people are assisted to return to independence and competence, but *above* which people are thought to be able to maintain themselves and to grow and develop through their own resources. In the Western European view, on the other hand, social welfare is seen as an open-ended continuum, on which any individual may at some time need to draw for his own level of creative and abundant life.

Thus, it may be said that the European *Weltanschauung* is comprehensive and concerns itself with the total structure of society. It includes the following ideas: (1) social welfare, as a state of social well-being, is viewed as an open-ended ideal, applicable to the population as a whole; (2) social services are seen as society's obligation to itself, and hence, as comprehensive and universal; (3) social work practice stresses the human and compassionate approach of letting people grow to develop their own potentials, rather than the intervention of professional experts. In contrast, in North America the dominant approach is that professional "experts" should help people cope, to attain or regain a "normal" level of functioning.

Related to these themes are contrasting North American and Western European views of the nature of public-voluntary relationships. Broadly speaking, in North America the welfare activities of government are seen as antithetical to those in the private or nongovernmental sector. In consequence, voluntary citizen participation is viewed as an ideological necessity, one that preserves a particular way of life, or shores up a particular political system. But in Western Europe this relationship is seen as essentially cooperative and complementary; voluntary citizen participation is evaluated in terms of the pragmatic benefits that might accrue.

The American view is predicated on a value orientation that holds the individual and his family responsible for the social ills that befall them. These ills must be cured, alleviated, or ameliorated primarily by the individual himself; by his relatives and friends only to the extent that the individual cannot cope. Society, through its agents in the public sector, may intervene only when other means have failed. If one looks at self-help organizations in North America from this perspective, it is not surprising that they have been essentially individually oriented, have not traditionally secured state or public support, and are considered essentially antithetical to government ventures.

On the other hand, in Western Europe it is held that the social ills befalling the individual arise from a faulty societal structure, thus placing the burden of responsibility for ameliorating or curing these ills on society as a whole. If the phenomenon of self-help is viewed from this perspective, it is not surprising that in *Western European countries much of the self-help undertaking is not only sanctioned by government, but is also actually encouraged and in many ways incorporated into the existing political structure.* One illustration is found in the area of preschool child development.

In North America preschool child development has typically been the domain of the private sector. In the majority of states in the United States and in most provinces in Canada, kindergartens are merely an additional grade in the educational system, grudgingly recognized as a right of the child and an added burden to public educational responsibility. The entire area of *early childhood development* and *preschool child care* has been left to the private sector, despite some limited and lukewarm public support. Programs like "Head Start" emerged in the 1960's in both North American countries to remedy or ameliorate the position of children of the poor and other minority groups. In the United States and Canada self-help groups supporting cooperative preschool or child-care activities have severe financial problems but receive only meager help from the public purse. Day-care is viewed as a *residual service* for particular groups of children whose parents are economically deprived.

In contrast, most West European countries acknowledge and act on the importance of early childhood development. The Montessori or Froebel School has been a fact of life in most of Western Europe for the past half-century. Even though most of the actual *services* are provided through self-help groups, the public purse finances practically 100 percent of the programs. In Denmark, for example, if a mothers' group bands together to establish a child development center or kindergarten in a new neighborhood, it is not required to prove that its members need to work, or be retained, or otherwise be out of the house, or that the children are economically, socially, and culturally deprived. Public support is assured for the self-help enterprise as long as it is efficiently set up and conducted.

This example shows that the self-help group in Europe is able to concentrate on the way in which social programs can best be carried out: there is little conflict over goals or what is conducive to people's well-being. In contrast, self-help groups in North America have to concentrate on changing social values and public attitudes in order to establish the validity of their programs in the first place. This results in a continuous battle; the achievement of a particular piece of legislation does not necessarily mean a change in social values and attitudes, but only a reluctant giving way on one point and a concomitant stiffening on others. It may be that in a pluralistic society—as both countries on the North American continent claim to be—agreement on the principles of a social philosophy for general well-being cannot be reached. But it is tragic and wasteful that much effort is spent on winning hard-fought singular campaigns, while the total victory remains elusive. This point may be illustrated further by a different type of self-help organization: the political activist.

A distinction can be made between the self-help group more or less homogeneous in its membership, which focuses on a single concern, and the heterogeneously composed self-help group, which may have many focuses of concern. The former concentrates on separate issues such as racial discrimination, housing, the war in Vietnam, air pollution, urban transportation, poverty, and so on. It marshals a good deal of commitment around its goal and often displays an initial spurt of energy and activity which rapidly peaks, then may diminish considerably. The diminution does not necessarily spell the disappearance of the group, but often results in a lessening of the initial drives and a shifting of group goals toward internal maintenance. Groups of this type seem more prevalent on the North American continent than in Western Europe.

In contrast, "multi-concern" or "multi-focus" self-help groups have broader social-philosophical goals, under which numerous issues can be subsumed. Such goals might include improving the quality of life or the humanization of a technocratically oriented society. Many self-help groups of this type are found in Europe. Both the earlier Provo and the present Kabouter movement in the Netherlands are cases in point. These Dutch groups started as protest movements against the dehumanization of society, but in contrast to the Hippie and Yippie movements in North America, which seem to have withdrawn from the political scene, the Kabouter movement has remained politically active to the extent that it now has members elected on both the local and national levels of government.

On the North American continent, the single-focus self-help groups often become isolated as social deviants. In contrast, in Western Europe, where the band of what is considered "normalcy'' is broader, the single-focus groups are not considered as outcasts. Male homosexuality is an example. Despite Prime Minister Pierre Trudeau's comment that "government does not have a place in the bedrooms of the nation," there is still a vast gulf between the social acceptance of homophile organizations in North America and in Europe. For example, the Dutch homophile group requested—and was granted—a royal charter for the society! In Western Europe, such self-help groups as homosexuals or ex-alcoholics, ex-drug addicts or ex-criminals, war protesters or anti-royalists are less stigmatized as "crackpots" or "social deviants," and consequently are less alienated from prevailing political organizations and structures than in North America. Disadvantaged groups in Western Europe have more access to social policy formulation and social planning processes than do their counterparts in North America.

In a milieu where basic social responsibility for the well-being of all members of society is not controversial, the self-help groups in Western Europe seem able to achieve the changes needed for the fulfillment of their goals. Visible and external protest activities do not seem essential to attainment of their goals. In North America, where a social philosophy that asserts society's responsibility for public well-being is still debatable, the self-help groups continue to be seen as gadflies, annoying to be sure, but in the long run, easily dealt with by co-optation or suppression.

20

Poland's Self-Help Rehabilitation Program

ALFRED H. KATZ

The factory was a huge and modern one on the outskirts of Warsaw, Poland. As we went from one well-lit, airy section to another, we saw amputees, paraplegics, deaf, and (as we were later told) mentally handicapped workers operating complicated drill press, stamping, and rolling machines; trimming plastic objects, packaging tablecloths, perfume, and soap; and adding features to rubber puppets and dolls.

This was the bustling Swit Cooperative (the name means "sunrise"), one of 420 constituents of the Polish Union of Invalid Cooperatives, a major and in some respects unique rehabilitation enterprise. Its uniqueness stems from its character as a self-help group. The disabled person and his family belong to and share in the enterprise and contribute to the formulation of its policies. Through it, many of their life needs may be met.

From a professional point of view, the cooperatives seem to provide incentives and a structure for the disabled person to participate and involve himself in his own recovery and rehabilitation and thereby contribute to solving the difficult problems of motivation and handicap.

While there were some prewar prototypes, most of the Invalid Cooperatives in Poland were established after World War II to supply work and vocational rehabilitation to the many citizens, both civilian and military, who were disabled in that devastated country. From the beginning the approach was to prepare disabled persons for work through a combination of treatment and training. Sheltered workshop placement for the severely disabled became a major move toward self-support in conditions suitable or adapted to the disabled individual's health and skills. Placement in the broader enterprises of the cooperatives and in the industrial life of the country were seen as intermediate and longer range goals.

Today a total of 420 Invalid Cooperatives run more than 3,000 workshops and enterprises engaged in production and services and, also, almost 4,000 shops, kiosks, etc. The number of persons employed by all of them exceeds 211,000 of whom 61,300—76.4 percent of the total—are disabled. It is hard to think of a vocational rehabilitation enterprise of such magnitude anywhere. About one-third of the persons vocationally rehabilitated

SOURCE: This article is based on the writer's article of the same name, *Rehabilitation Record*, vol. 5, no. 3 (May–June 1964), with an updating of statistical and other information from publications of the Union of Invalid Cooperatives, Warsaw, supplemented by subsequent visits to Poland in 1967, 1970, and 1973.

in Poland pass through the various facilities of the U.I.C.

The statutes of the Invalid Cooperatives provide that disabled personnel must make up at least 75 percent of the total; 25 percent can be able-bodied; the governing council and board follow the same principle.

The cooperatives are autonomous. Each is responsible for obtaining its own contracts, for employment practices, for training, and for marketing its products. Although based in a socialist country, the U.I.C. is *not* state owned or state managed. It obtains financial assistance from the state, including funds for capital development, remission of various taxes, and an allocation from members' social insurance contributions to aid in construction of medical facilities. U.I.C. also contracts with the state for the sale of some of its production, and its exports are an important source of Polish foreign currency balances. By law, the wage scales in the coops are on a par with those of comparable positions in other industries and include bonuses based upon a percentage of value of the work produced. In general, the cooperatives are thought in Poland to provide a highly desirable work milieu, since the bonuses for high production and other social benefits often increase the income of the disabled person above the levels of comparable workers.

Types of Workers and Production

At the end of 1971 the total personnel in the Invalid Cooperatives numbered 211,300. Production workshops employ 100,900; 34,800 are employed in a home-work system; 66,600 in services; and 9,000 in retail trade and other branches of the economy. Of this total, 161,300 suffer various disabilities. Among the latter are the following major categories:

Injuries of upper extremities	7,200
Injuries of lower extremities	17,300
Blind and visually impaired	14,600
Deaf and hearing impaired	7,300
Neurological diseases	8,100
Mental diseases	7,000
Rheumatological diseases	11,200
Mentally retarded persons	6,800

The disabled for the most part are employed in production workshops run by the cooperatives in these industries: metal, electrotechnical, chemical, rubber, building materials, glass, woodworking, paper, printing, textile, clothing, foodstuffs, leather and footwear, and brushmaking. Recent years have witnessed a great increase in the output of the cooperative metal, electrotechnical, electronic, and chemical industries. In the plants employing the blind, the traditional activity of brushmaking is being replaced by metal, electronics, and other types of work.

In the production facilities of the U.I.C. are also found many sheltered workshops for the disabled who are heavily afflicted and are unable to work in the ordinary production workshops of the cooperatives, but require special forms of training and care by skilled rehabilitation personnel. In 1971, 272 sheltered workshops employed 19,600 disabled, especially persons suffering from respiratory and mental diseases and mental retardation plus blind persons having an additional disability. We visited one sheltered workshop for former mental patients in Warsaw, where the concentration was on quiet forms of production such as bookbinding and assembling rather than on machine operation. This attractive physical setting accommodated about 80 workers and had a full-time psychiatrist as medical director.

In addition, the U.I.C. has an extensive social welfare program. Not only are vocational counseling and training and physical treatment provided, along with any necessary psychological counseling, but there are also varied kinds of material assistance to improve the disabled person's living conditions. These may take the form of loans or grants, help in obtaining housing, care of children or aged family members, or organized recreation and vacation services. Many of the cooperatives have constructed apartment units for their disabled members adjacent to the factories and workshops. We visited a center for blind workers in Cracow that had both attractive family units and a well-designed dormitory for single persons. The design of these facilities, which combine housing, work, and recreation, not only reflect adaptation to physical limitations, but also clearly facilitate a sense of community and neighborliness.

In 1971 more than 34,000 persons spent their holidays either at rest homes or "preventoria" of the U.I.C., situated in the most attractive localities in Poland, that is, the mountains, seaside, or lake district. Vacation provisions include members of the family as well as the employee. Much emphasis is placed on sports, for example, walking holidays, canoeing, outdoor camping, skiing, and so forth.

For the children of members, there is a network of summer and winter camps, day-care and nursery schools, clubs, community centers, and traveling schools.

More than 500 social workers help staff the cooperatives, rendering services centering on the individual needs of the disabled and their families, securing their maximum social insurance entitlements, relief in rent payments, appropriate prostheses and technical aids. The 35,000 homebound workers receive special attention, in efforts to overcome their social and educational isolation. There is regular visiting of homebound workers for these purposes, in addition to the delivery and pickup of work materials.

The U.I.C. has a central headquarters in Warsaw for overall administration, negotiations with the national government, consultation, and other central services. Here there is a special staff devoted to research in the economics, demography, and psychological aspects of rehabilitation. There is much interest in the psychology of rehabilitation and in studies of learning and motivation as well as in the applications of clinical studies and techniques of physical rehabilitation that are carried out in various cooperating medical centers.

As befits a federation, the U.I.C. has within it all manner of local and regional cooperatives set up on geographic lines and also includes cooperatives of and for special categories of the disabled, such as the blind or deaf.

Discussion

Motivation is a critical problem in vocational rehabilitation in the United States. Professionals express the fear that rehabilitation of the disabled in a milieu composed solely of the disabled might be a barrier to motivation toward full social rehabilitation. The experiences of the Polish cooperatives suggest that the opposite effect may be more probable. Their program seems to heighten motivation through the dynamics of social emulation.

Like the Abilities, Inc., program in this country, the Polish cooperatives provide a businesslike work milieu composed of others having disabilities, where it is not necessary to conceal or apologize for one's own disability. Further, they have been able to structure many means of social participation for their members. The latter are more than just "clients" or "production workers." The fact that the cooperatives are run as self-help groups with collective management provides members with a chance for testing more than their vocational skills and for receiving other forms of social gratification. They can be elected to local workshop boards and to supervisory councils of the many local, regional, and national governing bodies associated with the federation of cooperatives. They can and do participate in administration of the social welfare, housing, and recreational parts of the program.

Some current social theory has emphasized the importance of the self-help component in care, treatment, and motivation for the disabled individual. The Polish U.I.C. is providing further data that tend to validate this theory: the membership of the governing boards of the cooperatives is composed of a majority of disabled persons (the figure rises to as high as 80 percent in the upper governing boards). It reinforces a finding included in my study of parent associations for the handicapped (*Parents of the Handicapped,* Charles C Thomas, 1961) that the vesting of policy-making in the persons directly affected by a problem has a salutary effect upon the level of participation, interest, and cooperation in a remedial or therapeutic program. Of course, the marked cultural differences between Western capitalist countries and Poland must be borne in mind, since the "collective" philosophy of Polish life may be a profoundly important factor in the success of this sort of program.

The cultural, educational, and social activities carried on within the U.I.C. also embody the self-help principle. Clubs and community centers, artistic ensembles and hobby groups of all kinds emphasize the participation of members in activities of interest to them. Self-government and group self-determination programs and activities are continually stressed.

Thus we find in Poland, a large, well-rounded, and widely ramified program, in the form of a self-help group, which helps to vocationally rehabilitate one-third of the disabled people in the country and which makes a substantial contribution to Poland's economy. The impressive achievements of the U.I.C., which have been merely sketched above, indicate that we have here a most fertile laboratory for the study of the self-help component in rehabilitation services. Given the differences between United States and other Western culture patterns and Polish cultural patterns, it would seem highly desirable to conduct comparative research on the distinctive aspects and effects of the self-help structure and in particular on the outcomes of participation by the recipients of service in such a program.

> If we are not as cement, we shall be as sand.
> —Chinese proverb

21

Self-Help and Mutual Aid in the People's Republic of China

RUTH V. SIDEL

Before exploring the role of mutual aid and self-help in China today, it might be helpful first to describe some general characteristics of the country. China is an agricultural society; 80 percent of its population live in the rural areas and only 20 percent of the population live in the cities. In spite of the fact that more than 500 million of China's 750–800 million people are engaged in growing food crops, the feeding of this mammoth population has been an overwhelming problem for the Chinese over the centuries, for with almost 25 percent of the world's population to feed, China has only 7.8 percent of the world's cultivated land.[1]

Furthermore, despite the rapid growth of both heavy and light industry since 1949, China is still a poor country. Although mechanization has proceeded on China's communes, the peasants work long, hard hours doing much of their work by hand. And although substantial progress has been made in harnessing China's rivers and in irrigating areas formerly plagued by drought, much crop production is dependent on natural conditions. As recently as June 1973 *The New York Times* reported: "As for food, the weather pattern this year has been better than in 1972 but is still not good, and the crop outlook is uncertain. Drought has persisted in the north, while in the rich rice-growing provinces of the southeast the crops have been drowning."[2] China is still a society in which the vast majority of people are organized around the production of basic necessities.

But in 1949 at the time of the assumption of power by the Chinese Communists, which they call "Liberation," China was infinitely poorer. It was a disease-ridden nation in which famine and flood periodically took millions of lives. However, even though life in traditional China was a constant battle for survival, it was, nevertheless, a life that incorporated some elements of mutual aid.

Mutual Aid in Traditional China

The traditional Chinese family, while severely authoritarian and often cruel, functioned in some ways as a mini-mutual aid group. Children worked on the land with their parents and when a son married, he and his new wife traditionally lived with his mother and father. Offspring were reared and nourished so that they might one day care for their old and, in all likelihood, needy parents.[3]

Chinese rural society was primarily organized on the basis of kinship, work, religion, and other ties. Clans organized the villages and the villages, which were characterized more by self-organization than by organization from above, found links with nearby cities. Although agriculture was basically a family undertaking, extrafamilial elements of agricultural cooperation were used in farming. Some forms of mutual aid were especially prevalent in Northern Shensi Province, the area from which the Chinese Communists were to launch their revolution in the 1930's and 1940's.

Pien-kung was a form of cooperative labor among landowning farmers, which sometimes included the exchange of tools and animals. Because trust was essential to such cooperative endeavor, *pien-kung* was traditionally based on long-lasting personal relationships and was often limited to kinship groups. In addition, it was usually limited to rich rather than poor peasants.

Cha-kung was a second form of collective labor in which a group of workers, often ten or more, essentially work gangs who worked for a rich peasant or landlord, were hired out as a team. *Cha-kung* teams were organized and led by a boss (*kung-t'ou*) who acted as an intermediary between the workers and the landlord. *Cha-kung* was not really based on cooperative principles, but rather was highly organized, highly disciplined, and contained elements of exploitation of the peasants by the landlords.[4]

During the Communist administration of the Kiangsi Soviet in the south of China (1927–1934) prior to the Long March, the Communists attempted to organize village cooperatives. In 1934 they organized production cooperatives, consumption cooperatives, food cooperatives, and credit cooperatives.[5] But since much of the organization was from above rather than from below, it had limited success. It was not until the Yenan period that the Chinese Communists were able to utilize mutual aid with any substantial success. During this period they realized that unless the basic problem of the transformation of the traditional village and of the peasantry was solved, China's most crucial problem, that of food production, could not be solved. As Franz Schurmann has written, "Since little capital was available to invest in agriculture, the Chinese Communists decided to use organizational means to bring about a political and social transformation of rural society from which the needed economic revolution would develop."[6]

The Yenan Days (1935–1946)

The Communists began to learn techniques for organizing villages from below as well as from above. They had special problems in Shensi Province as the villages were small and the peasants lived near the edge of starvation. Not only was the food situation worsening but the Communists were also having problems with mass organization. During 1942 the Yenan leaders decided to launch a campaign for rural cooperativization.

The drive toward mutual aid was launched prior to spring planting in 1943. Although the statistics are difficult to evaluate, it appears that tens of thousands of peasants throughout the border region engaged in cooperative work from 1943 to 1945. Both the traditional forms of *pien-kung* and *cha-kung* were used experimentally. Although *pien-kung* groups involving seventy-five or more people were tried, the best results were with a group of about ten workers. The new forms of *pien-kung* insisted on obedience to an elected leader and on expanding membership beyond the narrow circle of friends and relatives, particularly to include poor peasants. Formerly *pien-kung* groups would disband after the planting or harvest season, but now an attempt was made to continue them throughout the entire production cycle.

A modified form of *cha-kung* was utilized particularly to assist immigrants who had no land or capital in claiming uncultivated lands. These new *cha-kung* teams often worked on their own behalf and divided among them the land which they had collectively farmed.[7]

An editorial, which appeared on January 25, 1943, in the newspaper *Chiehfang Jihpao* under the title "Let's Organize the Labor Force," best explains the philosophy behind the cooperativization efforts during the Yenan days:

> We know that it is vital in planting "not to violate the seasons." Whether you plant early or late can make a big difference, and harvesting late or early can also result in different yields. In

order not "to violate the seasons," if you simply rely on individual and scattered labor, your difficulties will be compounded. But it you make use of mutual aid in labor, the situation is very different. Take the men and animals of three to five households or seven to eight families and organize them; today everyone helps you plow, tomorrow everyone helps me plow—if that plot has too many weeds, then help that family hoe first; if that family's crops ripen first, then help them to harvest first. In pien-kung, not only do laborers rotate with each other, but three laborers can be exchanged for the work of one ox. Those who have labor give labor; those who have animals give animals. Those who have much give much; those who have little give little; human and animal power are put together. Thus, one can avoid violating the seasons and is able to plow in time, sow in time, hoe in time, and harvest in time.[8]

Thus, mutual aid was crucial for production needs, for efficient utilization of land, men, and animals, and for working in harmony with the seasons. But the Communists were also attempting to modify the thinking of the Shensi peasant. The editorial continues:

. . . Because everyone works together life is active, morale is high, and there is mutual stimulation, mutual competition, and no one wants to be behind the others. The driving pace of work is just as the masses say: "Work for Work, Everyone Exerts Himself to the Bone." In the end, mutual aid collective labor organization is a true organization of the masses, but also suits our Party and the work comrades of our mass groups; it educates the masses, and increases the spirit of mutual aid and solidarity among the masses.[9]

Mutual aid was being used as an organizational and an educational tool. It was used to expand the peasant's reference group from the relatively narrow one of the family or the clan to the wider one of his fellow peasants. As Mark Selden has stated, "The formation of mutual aid teams, the creation of a functioning socioeconomic network beyond the family unit, was a crucial step in bringing the peasant into a national state and a new society."[10]

Furthermore, the leaders clearly recognized that mutual aid, to be successful, needed to be based on the "voluntarism of the masses" and that high morale among the peasants was necessary to such voluntarism and to the success of the cooperativization efforts. They were also aware of the need for flexibility in developing cooperatives in the villages—flexibility in the number of cooperatives needed, flexibility in the number of people in each cooperative, and flexibility with regard to leadership. Cooperation in traditional rural China had, as we have noted, been based largely on kinship.[11] The Communists had to break through the kinship patterns in order to broaden the scope of collectivization, but they needed to use old kinship patterns in order to keep the support of the peasantry. The Communists knew, furthermore, that the key to organization was work and that the key on the part of the peasantry was recruitment of leadership from among indigenous leaders. They therefore recruited leaders of the village organizations into the movement. "Thus," states Schurmann, "young peasants, native to the village and leaders in work cooperation teams, were made into 'positivists' and finally taken into the party or other mass organizations. In this way the new cadres were simultaneously village team leaders and committed members of the party."[12]

The cooperative movement became further solidified with the integration of war and production. Mutual aid teams were often identical with units of the people's militia. The peasant was a soldier and the soldier a peasant. The slogan of that period was "Unity of Work and Arms." Soldiers were paid as though they were peasants working in the fields and in order to free up soldiers, women were encouraged to do the work normally done by men.

In order to understand more fully the importance of mutual aid during the Yenan days, it is also necessary to consider the concept of *tzu-li keng-sheng*, usually translated as "self-reliance" but more accurately translated as "regeneration through one's own efforts." *Tzu-li keng-sheng* has been a factor in Mao Tse-tung's philosophy on foreign policy since the mid-1930's when the Chinese were attempting to turn back the Japanese invaders. As early as December 27, 1935, Mao stated: "We Chinese have the spirit to fight the enemy to the last drop of our blood. The determination to recover our lost territory by our own efforts [*tzu-li keng-sheng*], and the ability to stand on our own feet in the family of nations."[13] The essential meaning of *tzu-li keng-sheng* is that the Chinese must transform China, must "stand up" in order to properly join the community of other nations.

The concept of *tzu-li keng-sheng* was simultaneously the key to the Communist domestic policy during the Yenan period. Laboring under both the enormous poverty of the Yenan area and the Japanese blockade, "relying upon one's own strength" (*yi kao tzu-chi li-liang*) became a solution for survival.

A resurgence of *tzu-li keng-sheng* was apparent in 1958 during the Greap Leap Forward when, on the domestic front, communes were formed in the hope of creating self-sufficient communities which would combine work and necessities of life and which would meet most of the needs of the commune members. The Sino-Soviet conflict, which became apparent in the late 1950's and which culminated in Soviet technicians being removed totally from China in 1960, gave additional impetus to *tzu-li keng-sheng*.

The Current Scene

A distinction must be drawn between "self-help" and "mutual aid" in China today. Because of the size of the country, the difficulty of central administration of all aspects of life, the perceived threat of war and consequent attempt to decentralize industry and expertise, the profound belief in mass participation, in learning through doing and in *tzu-li keng-sheng*, local groups have been encouraged to organize and to gradually accumulate, with little help from higher administrative levels, a reservoir of expertise and capital. This process is called "self-help."

The process whereby members of a peer group help one another to learn or to solve problems, personal or social, is called "mutual aid." Both mutual aid and self-help are often woven together in contemporary Chinese life—mutual aid, for example, is often part of a self-help process—but do seem to constitute two separate processes.

Self-Help and Mutual Aid in Urban Neighborhoods

Urban neighborhoods in China are organized, as are the rural areas, to promote decentralization and local participation. Cities are divided into districts and then are futher subdivided into "neighborhoods."

Shanghai City Proper, with a population of 10 million people, is divided into ten districts. The Kung Chiang Workers' New Village, located in the Yang-poo district of Shanghai, houses 64,000 people, 90 percent of whom are workers and their dependents. The New Village is further subdivided into residents' committees and each residents' committee is then divided into groups. The fifth residents' committee, for example, has a population of 7,000 and is divided into 88 groups, each apartment building housing approximately 80 people who comprise one group. Group leaders are selected by representatives of each family in the building who meet together to "discuss who is qualified." According to a member of the Kung Chiang revolutionary committee, "the group leader must learn Chairman Mao's work well and must have good relationships with his or her neighbors." The group leaders' responsibilities include settling disputes and helping people in times of difficulty. Social services are provided at both the group level and the residents' committee level either by those in charge or by neighbors for one another. If, for example, a woman delivers a baby and her husband is working out of the area, others in her block will help to care for her other children and help her to buy food. Or if an elderly widow needs to be brought to the hospital and has no family to assist her, her neighbors, group leaders, or members of her residents' committee will come to her aid. One elderly retired textile worker, when asked if she had many friends in her neighborhood, replied, "All the people here are my friends; we all help each other."

It must be stated clearly, however, that the residents' committees are organized by the neighborhood committees and function under their watchful eye. While much of the mutual aid that occurs within the urban residents' committees and groups is spontaneous, much is carefully planned, orchestrated to meet the needs of the people and to encourage cooperation and mutual concern. Even after a residents' committee is organized and functioning, it remains under the guidance of a member of the neighborhood committee.

During the Great Leap Forward of 1958 neighborhood factories were organized utilizing the dependents of urban factory workers who had remained out of the labor force. These neighborhood factories were usually rudimentary efforts with little equipment, primitive workshops, and untrained housewives as workers. The workers earned low wages at the start and it was expected that as the factory earned more money, the workers' earnings would increase.

The Ching Nian Lu Printing and Binding Factory in Sian is another example of self-reliance and collective effort at work in the urban scene. In 1966 at the beginning of the Cultural Revolution, the slogan "Grasp the Revolution and Promote Production" was prominent. The housewives of the urban commune of Ching Nian decided that they wished to go to work and so informed their local residents' committee. Members of the residents' committee found a larger factory nearby which needed work done, and five of the original fifteen housewives went to the factory for one month to learn the work. The remaining ten prepared rudimentary tools and set up a space to work under a roof in the neighborhood. When the group that was trained at the larger factory returned to the neighborhood, they trained the remaining workers. At the beginning they worked by hand, but as their earnings grew they were able to purchase a few small machines.

By the fall of 1972, thirty-seven workers were working in the local factory. Production has increased twelvefold since 1966, and the value of their output had increased five times over last year. They proudly told of overfulfilling the tasks set for them this year by the urban commune committee. Originally the workers had earned 7 yuan per month; in 1972 they earned an average salary of 35 yuan per month. As has been the case since the factory's inception, the workers are paid out of factory earnings and any money left over is used to enlarge the factory. The factory also provides a cooperative health program and handles the welfare needs of the workers. Thus the workers' salaries rise in direct proportion to their production with no aid from the local neighborhood organization, the city of Sian, or the larger factory other than the original provision of space, rudimentary tools, and a training period at the larger factory.

Self-Help on the Communes

China's communes are the lowest level of rural state power. They are divided into production brigades and further subdivided into production teams, which frequently consist of only thirty or forty families who live close to one another and are, in fact, often related to one another. The team is roughly equivalent to the traditional Chinese village. Each level of rural organization is encouraged to make decisions locally whenever possible, to rely on collective leadership, to elicit the participation of the "mass," and to raise their economic level using "self-reliance" and "hard work."

The Tachai Brigade, for example, is famous throughout China. The words "In Agriculture, Learn from Tachai" are written on walls, on banners, on houses, and on hillsides throughout the country. Tachai is a small collection of villages in Hsiang County, Shansi Province, in the northern part of China, a mountainous area where the hills are made of brown loess and which until recent times was among the poorest and least cultivatable land in all China. Four hundred thirty people live in an area of 790 *mu,* a little over 130 acres.

Before Liberation seventy-three families lived where this brigade is now situated. In spite of immense poverty, Tachai's fame began as early as 1945 when Hsiang County was liberated from Japanese rule by the Eighth Route Army. The Communists instituted land reform and formed cooperative groups. In 1953 they set up an agricultural cooperative in which the peasants jointly owned the land but maintained private ownership over their own tools. At first only thirty families joined the cooperative, but when the others saw the progress made by the cooperative, more families joined. In 1958 they set up the first People's Commune in their country.

During the late 1950's and early 1960's the peasants of Tachai built a dam, cultivated new plots, and built stone and mud walls to protect the terraced fields on the hillsides. When they first built the walls, rain washed them away. They then rebuilt them, but heavy rains washed them away once again. After much discussion among the peasants, they rebuilt the walls still higher and more solidly and in 1963 were expecting a good harvest. However, in August tragedy struck Tachai. It rained for seven days and seven nights. The floods were so severe that 97 percent of the houses collapsed and 90 percent of the crops were destroyed.

When the rain finally stopped, the people of Tachai gathered together to decide their course of action. The central government sent grain and money immediately for the relief of the inhabitants. But after much discussion and debate the people and the leadership of Tachai decided on three "don't wants": they didn't want money; they didn't want grain; and they didn't want materials. They returned all three. The people of Tachai decided that they had to rebuild their brigade with their own hard work and through self-reliance. Men, women, and students helped to rebuild the walls which had been destroyed by the floods, to replant and recultivate the fields, and to rebuild the homes. In spite of the tragic floods Tachai had a good harvest the following year. The people of Tachai had lived in old mud caves built into the hillside before the floods. Now, borrowing money from the peasants themselves rather than asking for state aid, they built homes out of heavy stone and packed earth. No longer built into the hillsides, they are sturdy and protected from floods. By 1971 Tachai had a record production of rice and grain and was famous throughout the country because of the spirit and insistence of its people on rebuilding their brigade themselves.

Mutual Aid among Children

Children from the ages of two or three are taught the words of Mao Tse-tung, that they must "care for each other, love and help each other." They are encouraged to pick each other up when one falls down, to button one another's jackets in the winter, to help each other in academic studies and in sports events. This is clearly the beginning of lifelong teaching to live cooperatively.

Mutual Aid in Therapeutic Settings

Mutual aid is utilized in the treatment of mental patients. Patients are paired, sicker patients with healthier patients, so that the former can be helped by the latter. Patients also participate in regular study sessions, using the writings of Mao Tse-tung to analyze their own illnesses and points of view and to "remold their attitudes."

Criticism and self-criticism sessions have been part of the Chinese Communist remolding of attitudes since the 1930's. Group sessions in which all members of the group analyze the attitudes and behavior of any one member, while he simultaneously attempts to criticize himself, are used as part of a rehabilitation of persons who may be criminals, or simply cadres or professionals who need to reexamine their basic attitudes.

Summary

Although China is a country in which the basic needs of the individual for food, shelter, and work are met by the society, it is nevertheless a society in which the masses of people are urged to participate actively. Chinese citizens are organized through their rural communes, their urban neighborhoods, and their places of work to engage in self-help and/or mutual aid to accomplish economic goals, therapeutic goals, and educational goals, to help people acquire a mastery over their environment, and to teach and promote a value system based on cooperation.

Several characteristics of these self-help or mutual aid groups in China must be stressed.

1 | Self-help and mutual aid frequently stem from necessity. China still does not have the economic resources to finance and equip all facets of the economy; thus neighborhood factories struggling to upgrade their machinery, their know-how, and their products are, at least in part, operating out of current economic realities.

2 | Self-help and mutual aid groups in China are organized and sponsored by those in positions of power. While the origins of these groups may have been, in some cases, spontaneous, and while indigenous leadership is most frequently utilized, the involvement and encouragement of the authorities nevertheless is ongoing.

3 | Many self-help groups, though initially organized in times of economic crisis or natural disaster, frequently continue to function over long periods of time. This is not the case, however, in transient therapeutic settings such as mental hospitals or prisons where the duration of the group is short.

4 | Within self-help groups, nonprofessionals often assume roles generally played elsewhere by professionals—for example, in psychiatric hospitals where one patient is helping another, or in the "Each one teach one" literacy drive of the 1950's when small children taught their parents and grandparents to read characters and peasants taught each other.

5 | Crucial in this process of self-help and mutual aid as it is seen in China is the learning process which each individual experiences as he participates in such a group. Through participating, through problem-solving, through experimenting, the Chinese citizen acquires a more accurate picture of the world around him, its problems and ways of solving those problems. He simultaneously gains a new image of himself—one in which he is an active agent shaping his own destiny rather than a passive pawn for others to manipulate. This profound belief that knowledge originates from personal experience has been an intrinsic component of Chinese Communism since the Yenan days. In Mao's words, written in 1937: "Whoever wants to know a thing has no way of doing so except by coming into contact with it, that is, by living (practicing) in its environment. . . . If you want knowledge, you must take part in changing reality."[14]

Part VII

Summary
and
Conclusions

22

Self-Help Groups and the Organized Society: A Stocktaking and Excursus

All living creatures, said Kenneth Burke, are critics. They seek security, sustenance, and room to grow. If these are not available or are denied to them, the living become critics and react against the depriving forces of the environment.

When human beings cannot find a place in the society and become critics, society often labels and derogates them as deviants or misfits. It is natural then for the stigmatized and disadvantaged to find support among fellow sufferers or victims. When other people—the so-called normals—don't understand one's viewpoint on the world, life lacks meaning. Thus, when society does not help suffering or needy people, they seek solace from others with the same complaint, even though there may be little else in common.

So groups are formed with a focus on some common dissatisfactions or deprivations; the voices are strengthened and raised in criticism; the existence of the group in its attempt to find its own ways to cope is a living attack on the values of the society.

Implicit in every self-help group, then, including those focused on individual adaptation, is a criticism of lacks or failures of the larger society. All the groups discussed in this book show by their very existence that they have found something lacking in the American society of the fifties, sixties, and seventies. For some of the groups, like sections of the Women's Movement and Operation Bootstrap, the criticism of the society is strong and explicit. These groups have reacted to the larger society's discrimination, oppression, and lack of nurturance by rejecting its values, its formal structures, and many of its practices.

The previous chapters have shown how even the least "successful" or effective self-help groups help give their members an anchorage, a reference point; many additionally give social support and companionship; some make possible real personal fulfillment and aid participants in establishing a changed and acceptable identity. Such groups as Camphill, X-Kalay and Synanon, communes, and some sections of the Women's Movement even make possible an alternative way of living.

As we consider what the self-help groups portend, the functions that they perform for their members should be kept in mind. The groups develop and exist in a changing social context. To the extent that the rate of change in people's values and beliefs outruns that of society's institutions, and as the latter are increasingly perceived as inflexible and unnurturant, self-help groups will continue to be founded and to grow. It is obvious that technological-political developments occur much more rapidly than social institutions change, so that the dehumanizing and alienating trends of our society will probably be ascendant for a long time.

Forecasting social change in this way is risky business, but the future is at least partly predicted by past and present trends. And without evidence to the contrary, it appears that those alienating trends of the recent past and present that brought the groups into being and that sustain them will probably continue and may intensify in American society.

Some sociologists argue that the self-help groups are simply another transient kind of informal social organization, interesting enough perhaps, but not very important, and certainly lacking in staying power. Or, the groups are viewed, as by Edward Sagarin, as a phenomenon of a pluralistic American society, which is large and secure enough to legitimize a place for organizations of deviants, even though some of them now have added the uncomfortable new twist of social activism.

Sagarin's description of the groups, while generally accurate, does not cut deeply enough. For their members, participating in the kind of self-help groups we have described is different and has more consequences than participating in social reform or political movements. Many self-help groups aim specifically to heighten their individual members' awareness and consciousness of themselves and their social relationships. Because of this approach, such groups' critiques of existing social forms and values often go deeper than those of other movements' in that they are not merely intellectual, but are coupled with emotional regeneration or growth. The consequences for members may thus be more lasting though less immediately apparent. Speaking very broadly, some self-help groups create and educate a generation of self-conscious critics, of iconoclasts, and sometimes of revolutionaries—people who have learned what it is they want from life and who have learned how to attain it despite the rigidities or exclusions of the social structure.

It is, perhaps, theoretically possible that the larger society will somehow transform itself, become more flexible and nurturant so that the needs for such groups will die out. Perhaps—but this seems very doubtful.

In thinking of the future—apocalyptic visions apart—it may be useful to try to differentiate between the probable futures of different kinds of self-help groups. Single-purpose groups like certain welfare rights organizations might fade out if their immediate objective of scrapping the welfare system and replacing it by a more humane, efficient, and less degrading one were achieved. But then a dialectical process would surely ensue: having come together, gained strength through organization, learned to work on common problems, welfare rights organization members would probably stay in motion to combat the inadequacies of the "new" system.

The "anonymous" groups in their various forms will probably continue, so long as addictions represent for many troubled persons a way of finding relief from, or coping with, the pressures of society. But here one can perhaps anticipate the "magic bullet" solution—a pill or injection that will somehow cure the cravings for alcohol or other dependency-creating chemicals. (Much current research is pointed in that direction.) But such a solution would not overcome the underlying sociopsychological difficulties that have accompanied the physiological craving. Self-change—what we have termed personal regeneration—accompanied by change in social institutions is the only reliable preventive. Some "anonymous" groups, of course, do not deal with addictions at all—Schizophrenics Anonymous is a case in point, since schizophrenia, whatever its ultimate etiology, is a disease or several diseases whose victims have presumably not had the choice of whether or not to acquire it.* And Gamblers Anonymous deals with a sociopsychological addiction, not a physiological one.

The methodology of the "anonymous" groups, as we have seen, partakes of religion, Couéism, and other simplistic self-improvement methods, which have been recurrently discovered

---

*It is of interest that Schizophrenics Anonymous, U.S.A., in the summer of 1972 dissolved itself as a self-help group and has become a foundation supporting medical research (see *Medical Opinion*, June 1972). However, the Canadian Schizophrenics Anonymous is continuing in its original form.

and used many times in human history. But there is an additional element, pioneered by A.A. and adopted by others, the sponsor or "buddy" system, which provides to the novitiate an experienced counselor, who has himself been successful in overcoming the addiction, whenever temptation or inducement arises. This device for guaranteeing reliable personal support round-the-clock is indeed a useful addition to the social relationships available in a fragmented and depersonalized society and represents a social innovation that could be widely applied.

The future of the self-help groups that provide for the heightening of awareness (consciousness-raising), self-fulfillment, and/or alternative life-styles are far more complex and difficult to analyze. Their mirror-image, love-hate relationship with the dominant society is complex—to know if and how they will evolve is as impossible as to know, in any true sense, how the larger society will grow and change. Kurt Back,[1] and other students of the "sensitivity" training movement and its widely proliferating forms of "instant therapy" growth centers like Esalen, believe that their positive features may be incorporated into the therapeutic armory of established professional "helpers." Back sees the organizational side of the movement as a transient by-product of middle-class affluence and leisure.

Yet, although in the past in many places such groups have arisen and flourished for a while and then declined as social conditions changed, it does not seem likely that this will be the fate of those contemporary groups that have emphasized the creation of alternative social institutions. The Women's Movement, Camphill Villages, Operation Bootstrap, some communes built around religious beliefs or other strong central themes, all seem likely to endure because their premises and organizational forms meet the continuing needs of many persons. Even if they do not endure as formal organizations, they have helped thousands of people to reach new states of self-awareness and self-confidence, to find new freedoms, and to clarify their ideas about themselves, the society, the ways in which they want to and can live.

It isn't necessary to adopt the romanticism of Charles Reich's *Greening of America* to believe that such people will inevitably influence whatever social institutions they come into contact with —their impact on the larger society will surely be felt, although we cannot measure just how. We suggest, though, that their heightening of self-consciousness and self-knowledge leads to an enhanced social competence, not necessarily dependent on the panoply of formal structures. And if the primary institutions of family and workplace and the rest are not satisfying, noncompetitive small groups for social interaction and support will continue to be sought and created.

A Balance Sheet

So much for the future. How can we assess the effects of the groups here and now? Is there, in fact, more than hearsay or self-serving testimony from the groups themselves that suggests they are doing something useful for their members? Are they sometimes harmful to individuals or don't they matter very much at all? Answers to these questions are not easy to find—data and research are scanty, methodological difficulties severe—but some exist. In the first place, it certainly seems true, as is often charged, that some self-help groups habitually exaggerate their own numbers, their influence on the public, and their helpfulness to their members.

But even in the absence of convincing "objective" studies, that many people have been helped by them seems beyond dispute. Synanon, Recovery, Inc., A.A., and other "anonymous" groups have clearly brought personal benefits to many of their member-participants. Despite their high rates of turnover and attrition, the same can be said of many communes. It is known that this kind of group cannot and does not help everyone who comes to them; many people drop away from them after one or a few contacts. Synanon, which keeps some statistics, has been reluctant to publish or share them with investigators, perhaps because its dropout rate is high. The other groups generally do not keep statistics; few "objective" studies have been performed on them (a few have been included in this volume) and assessment efforts must be largely pieced together from observations, case histories, official reports—perhaps best of all, by talking with members and attending meetings. All evidence we have been able to obtain from these sources confirm the groups' values to their members.

Another way of evaluating the significance of the groups is to look at their impact on public attitudes and understanding. Does the public, in fact, understand more and have a more accepting attitude toward alcoholism, drug abuse, other addictions, mental illness, as a result of the activities of the self-help groups in those fields? It is not easy to answer this question—again, there are few data—but it is probably true that public attitudes toward these problems are now more liberal and less punitive, more understanding that social forces rather than mere individual dereliction are the prime movers. That a large, vague, and uneven shift of public attitudes has occurred vis-à-vis such "social deviants" seems evident; it is probable that the self-help groups, particularly the larger and better publicized ones, have contributed to this shift, but in what proportions and in what specific ways is unknown. Sagarin believes that all the self-help groups have been given much support and excellent treatment by the media—and that this has facilitated their influence on the public. While the first assertion may be true for some cases, it is certainly not true for all, and, even so, it seems questionable that mere exposure in the press, TV, radio, and so forth would influence public attitudes very much, except to convince the already convinced—to preach to the converted.

In fact, the publicity the groups get through the media, particularly TV, seems a mixed blessing. While quite a lot of money may be raised in this way, the media set their own requirements; stigma is often magnified, not reduced, when members are presented as appealing objects worthy of charity, perhaps of pity, but are not accorded full dignity, respect, and acceptance as persons. Magnifying the "deviance" or difference in the interests of titillating the public, or of newsworthiness, or highlighting an individual member's accomplishments, may not serve or may conflict with the organization's basic educational aims. Thus, a group of ex-mental patients may be presented with sympathetic intent, but in a way that emphasizes their sickness, not their humanity and their rights as persons; their disabilities and problems, not the things they can do for themselves. True public education requires much more than merely blazoning the spectacular aspects of personality or culturally stereotyped stigmas of deviance or protest. Tom Wolfe's phrase "radical chic" comes to mind—in a slightly different context—when talk shows parade Gay Lib, Synanon, or Women's Liberation members for half an hour of superficial questioning. The record of the media is far from bad, but the essential *seriousness* of the groups is hardly emphasized by such presentations.

It is true, of course, that the older and more professionalized type of self-help group, such as the United Cerebral Palsy Associations with its battery of staff, fund-raisers, and P.R. men, exploits the media as often, as thoroughly, and with the same aims as other fund-raising groups, and that this repetition and reinforcement does make an impact.

But the less professionalized and nonprofessionalized groups lack such resources, and their contacts with the public through communications media are sporadic and unsustained.

Some self-help groups that deal in very broad social questions —the welfare rights organization is an example—are clearly interested in using all available means of education to bring their message home, but education, understanding, and support from the public are not their specific purpose, although these purposes are not rejected if incidentally achieved. These groups are notably self-centered, centripetal in effect, interested in their members as such and the advancement of their cause, and much less so in the impression they make on the outside world.

Sagarin and others have raised the possibility that the groups magnify the isolation of their members from the "mainstream," and that in so doing they increase the members' sense of alienation and rejection. Again, there are few data to support or deny this idea, but on theoretical grounds, at least, it does not seem a valid criticism.

Perhaps the whole idea of a "mainstream" in the United States circa 1975 is a fiction. Almost half a century has passed since Sinclair Lewis wrote a famous series of novels about conformist middle-level America. Many of the groups we have described reject Main Street or "mainstream" values in practice; many so-called normal and conforming citizens do so privately. The comfortable pieties of Zenith, Illinois, in the 1920's have been irretrievably shattered and there are now at least several "mainstreams."

The notion that the groups tend further to segregate their members does not seem to stand up; first, because the isolation or exclusion, partial or complete, of participants in these groups has already been brought about by and within the larger society. Second, because membership in all these groups is entirely voluntary —membership is an act of will and choice—and no one who chooses or is able to find himself in the larger society need join. And, third, if participation in the groups does, as we believe, tend to heighten social competence, then the individual is enabled thereby to attain the kind of social satisfactions that he desires.

It is true, of course, that a notable minority of groups have decided to "go it alone." The most striking example we know of a self-help group that has taken this course is Operation Bootstrap in Los Angeles. Although helped initially with money and technical guidance from sympathetic businessmen, Bootstrap decided that the general white society offers no real possibilities for living in a human way to poor black people. Therefore, it has started to create its own alternative institutions. As Lou Smith's article indicates, having founded and learned how to run a successful business, the Bootstrap group is now planning to set up a school, a day-care center, medical clinics, and ultimately housing projects and a university.

Bootstrap specifically rejects the assistance of white *professionals*, regarding their contributions (there may be a few exceptions) either as expressions of "domestic colonialism" or as simply irrelevant to what black people need and can use. Thus Bootstrap is guided by a refusal to accept any institutional aid from the white power structure—federal antipoverty money was rejected on principle; in this Lou Smith differed sharply from other black leaders. The refusal of federal-state funds by Bootstrap is not unique; Synanon has also done so.

This brings us to the key question of integration: What is the degree of cooperation between the self-help groups and other institutions and organizations of the larger society? It would be easy and acceptable to "liberal" dogma to suggest that integration is an aim of the groups, and that it will probably occur once they have consolidated group identities through a period of separatism. But, in fact, this does not seem likely to occur; it is much more likely that in a pluralistic society they will continue as important groups for their own members, maintaining their uniqueness and contributing in their particular fashion to the world.

In this connection, self-help groups contrast notably with the *formal* institutions set up by society as "overseers of the poor" (the antique phrase) or, in more modern idiom, "caretakers" or "helping professionals."

While they differ greatly, in the best self-help groups there is an informality, an accessibility, an openness that challenges the artificiality and self-protective character of "professional" approaches in the human services. Dumont[2] reminds us that "a broad array of nonresidential, community-based, self-help activities are developing throughout the nation. Hotlines, drop-in centers, runaway houses, free clinics, and a host of other acute social and health service facilities, all relying on youthful, indigenous and nonprofessional staffs with the backup, training, and support of occasional professionals. Young people in trouble with drugs have been turning to facilities with such names as 'The Open Door,' 'The Kool Aid,' 'Bridge,' 'Help,' 'Concern,' 'Sanctuary,' 'Place,' to be talked down from a bad trip, for a meal, or a place to sleep, or because of a feared overdose, as a way of getting back home, or just for someone to talk to."

These self-help programs powerfully demonstrate that human service systems can provide, not relationships of super and subordination (symbolized by the mysterious and omniscient white-coated M.D.), but relationships where there is no vast or exploitative gap between giver and recipient of help but mutuality and interchange on a fully human level.

What the self-help groups also portend, then, are new ways of helping, of dealing with fellow human beings, of learning how to get along, organize, and communicate with peers.

Before concluding this assessment, it should also be said, and is easily demonstrable, that self-help groups have made tangible and material contributions to the larger society, not merely in the spheres of personal regeneration and public attitude change. A balance sheet would show that they also render many significant social services to their members, that they have stimulated research and professional training, have helped to achieve beneficial legislation, and in general have moved the broader society to more enlightened and human attitudes and policies toward the stigmatized. In giving to the individual member, self-help groups have thus also given to the larger society.

In their newer forms, such as communes, self-help groups interestingly demonstrate ways of living that hark back in many aspects to traditional American values—a Christian communal tradition, hard work, and respect for the soil, evoking the agrarian heritage, grass-roots decision-making in the populist tradition.

Many persons who enter and stick with a group such as those described in this volume have found a road to survival, a useful way of adapting to a complex and rapidly changing society. And this "acculturation" has been achieved through personal, indigenous effort, separate from the massive structures of government or formal institutions.

Self-help groups, then, offer an opportunity for personal socialization to "outsiders," to stigmatized and handicapped persons, in a society paradoxically rife with groups, organizations, and recreational outlets, but perceived as impersonal, alienating, and nonparticipatory by many citizens.

Despite its promises of pluralism and of the forms of political democracy, this society has few means of guaranteeing satisfactory identity achievement. Self-help groups may be seen as one means of vivifying the Jeffersonian ideal—of the decentralization of institutions allied to humanization. Their embodiment of this ideal points to a way of living in "postindustrial society."

In the contemporary "welfare" state, there is a great deal of impersonality in giving and receiving aid. As Harold Wilensky and Charles Lebeaux remind us:[3]

Modern social welfare has really to be thought of as help given to the stranger, not to the person who by reason of personal bond commands it without asking. It assumes a degree of social distance between helped and helper.

To eliminate or reduce this "distance" is a necessity for many people, who find that self-help groups nourish their personal growth and survival. *The Strength in Us* is not merely a pious or hopeful catchphrase but a program for being able to deal with a complicated and often bitter social reality.

"America," wrote Walt Whitman, "is promises." In the re-evaluation of existing social values and norms that is taking place irreversibly in America today, it is not too much to say that the self-help groups are prodding the troubled giant to achieve its many-times aborted promises. The self-help groups represent, among other things, a transitional phase to a less uniform, less conforming, and more open society, in which individual Americans will insist in attaining a wider range of choices about how their lives are to be lived.

Yet, important as these contributions are, the significance of the self-help phenomenon may be even wider. It is not too visionary also to see the groups as a vehicle for *social* change, of an untapped and even unimagined potency. If the phrase *people in action on their own behalf* sums up the guiding motif of politics in the second half of the twentieth century, then the very form and thrust of the self-help movement is syntonic to political and social change. We have barely realized the implications and the promises of the "participatory democracy" that the Founding Fathers envisioned and wrote into the blueprints of their brave new world and that populist movements periodically seek to revive. Many disillusioning aberrations and corruptions of the political process and political leaders have turned away the young, the sensitive, and the idealistic so that today *all* forms of political action are disdained or suspected. Hundreds of the counter-cultural flowers that bloomed in the 1960's, many promising "movements" and counter-forces, have withered and vanished from the scene.

Yet the climate, the special demon, the *spirit* of self-help groups seems congruent also with this broad movement for social change. Self-help groups may be able to thrust the movement forward to whatever presently unimaginable embodiments of the good society lie on the near—not impossibly far-off—shores of cooperative social action. "Not mine for me, but ours for us."

Notes
and
References

1 | Introduction: Why Self-Help?
1. Theodore Roszak, *The Making of a Counter-Culture* (New York: Doubleday, 1969), p. 23.
2. Wilhelm Reich, *The Mass Psychology of Fascism* (New York: Farrar, Straus and Giroux, 1971), p. 211.
3. Roszak, *op. cit.*, p. 47.
4. Erving Goffman, *Stigma: Notes on the Management of Spoiled Identities* (Englewood Cliffs, N. J.: Prentice-Hall, 1963).

2 | Self-Help and Mutual Aid in History
1. J. F. De Jongh, "Self-Help in Modern Society," in G. R. B. Billimoria and S. D. Patel, *Self-Help in Social Welfare, Proceedings of the Seventh International Conference of Social Work, Toronto, June-July 1954* (Bombay, India: The South-East Asia Regional Office, International Conference of Social Work, 1954), p. 51.
2. Petr Kropotkin, *Mutual Aid: A Factor of Evolution* (Boston: Extending Horizons Books, 1955), pp. 119–120.
3. M. Rooff, *Voluntary Societies and Social Policy* (London: Routledge & Kegan Paul, 1957), pp. 3–4.
4. Lord Beveridge, *Voluntary Action. A Report on Methods of Social Advance* (New York: Macmillan, 1948), p. 62.
5. E. P. Roy, *Cooperatives: Today and Tomorrow* (Danville, Ill.: The Interstate Printers and Publishers, Inc., 1964), Chap. 3.
6. C. M. Wieting, *The Progress of Cooperatives* (New York: Harper & Row, 1952), p. 7.
7. E. Cowling, *Co-operatives in America: Their Past, Present and Future* (New York: Coward-McCann, 1943).
8. John R. Commons, *History of Labour in the United States*, 4 vols. (New York: Macmillan, 1961).
9. Mary R. Beard, *American Labor Movement* (New York: Arno Press, 1939).
10. Frank Adams, *Education for Social Change*, pamphlet published by the Highlander Folk School, Knoxville, Tenn. (March 1971).

3 | Self-Help as a Social Movement
1. Hans Toch, *The Social Psychology of Social Movements* (Indianapolis and New York: Bobbs-Merrill, 1965).
2. Alfred H. Katz, "Self-Help Organizations and Volunteer Participation in Social Welfare," *Social Work*, vol. 15, no. 1 (January 1970).
3. "Background Information on the Fellowship of Alcoholics Anonymous," pamphlet issued by the General Service Office of A.A. (New York City, 1966).
4. "Their Brothers' Keepers" (Berkeley, Calif.: Pacific School of Religion, 1963, mimeographed).
5. See vol. 1, no. 1 newsletter of the National Welfare Rights Organization (April 1969), as well as bulletin of April 1970. In June 1972 there were welfare rights groups in twenty Canadian cities.
6. William B. Cameron, *Modern Social Movements: A Sociological Outline* (New York: Random House, 1966), p. 8.

7. Herbert Blumer, *New Outline of the Principles of Sociology,* ed. by A. M. Lee (New York: Barnes and Noble, 1951), pp. 199–220.

8. Ralph H. Turner, "The Theme of Contemporary Social Movements," *British Journal of Sociology,* vol. 20 (December 1969).

9. Katz, *op. cit.,* p. 52.

10. Edward Sagarin, *Odd Man In: Societies of Deviants in America* (New York: Quadrangle Books, 1969).

11. Cameron, *op. cit.,* p. 10.

12. Toch, *op. cit.,* pp. 75–85.

13. Eugene I. Bender, "The Citizen as Emotional Activist: An Appraisal of Self-Help Groups in North America," in *Canada's Mental Health,* vol. XIX, no. 2 (March-April 1971).

4 | Toward a Classification of Self-Help Groups

1. *An Introduction to Parents Anonymous,* Redondo Beach, California, 1971. This brochure issued by the group poses the question as to how P.A. began and says: "Literally, out of desperation over lack of treatment sources became the motivation factor for a child abuser to start this program."

2. Edward Sagarin, "Voluntary Associations Among Social Deviants," *Criminologia,* vol. V (May 1967), pp. 8–22.

5 | Therapeutic Type: Recovery, Inc.

1. *Recovery Reporter,* vol. 31 (July-August 1968), p. 4.

2. Alfred H. Katz, "Self-Help Groups," in H. L. Lurie (ed.), Encyclopedia of Social Work, 15th issue (New York: National Association of Social Workers, 1965).

3. Henry Wechsler, "The Self-Help Organization in the Mental Health Field: Recovery, Inc., A Case Study," *Journal of Nervous and Mental Disorders,* vol. 130 (1960), pp. 297–314.

4. O. Hobart Mowrer, *The New Group Therapy* (Princeton, N.J.: Van Nostrand, 1964).

5. Mrs. Abraham A. Low, *How a Panel Example Should Be Constructed* (copyright 1955).

6. Abraham A. Low, *Mental Health Through Will-Training,* 14th ed. (Boston: Christopher Publishing House, 1966).

7. *Ibid.*

8. *Ibid.*

9. State of California, Department of Mental Hygiene, Bureau of Biostatistics, Bulletin 45, Part I, Tables 17, 19 (1966).

10. *Ibid.*

11. *Ibid.*

12. U.S. Bureau of the Census, Statistical Abstract of the United States: 1961 (82nd ed.), Washington, D.C., 1961.

13. *Ibid.*

14. *Ibid.*

15. State of California, *op. cit.*

16. Frank Riessman, "The 'Helper' Therapy Principle," *Social Work*, vol. 10 (1965), pp. 27–32.

17. Donald T. Lee, "Recovery, Inc.: A Well Role Model," *The Quarterly of Camarillo*, vol. 2 (1966), pp. 35–36.

18. Abraham A. Low, *Lectures to Relatives of Former Patients* (Boston: Christopher Publishing House, 1967).

7 | "Rock-Bottom Haven" Type: X-Kalay

1. John B. Enright, "Synanon: A Challenge to Middle-Class Views of Mental Health," in *Community Psychology and Mental Health: Perspectives and Challenges*, edited by Daniel Adelson and Betty L. Kalis (Scranton, Pennsylvania: Chandler Publishing Company, 1970), pp. 238–261.

2. Peter Collier, "The Houses of Synanon," *Ramparts*, vol. 6, no. 3 (October, 1967), 93–100.

8 | Some Mixed Forms of Self-Help Groups

1. Elizabeth T. Harris, "Parents without Partners, Inc.: A Resource for Clients," *Social Work*, vol. 11, no. 2 (April 1966), 92–98.

2. *Ibid.*

3. As of this writing, PWP has under consideration a change of name to "Single Parents, International" to give a more positive connotation for prospective members.

4. *Fortune News* (February 1972), p. 5.

5. *Ibid.*

6. Nancy Hodgkin, in *New Society* (London, September 18, 1969).

9 | Participation Patterns and Benefits of Membership in a Self-Help Organization of Stutterers

1. Edwin M. Lemert, "Sociological Perspective," in Joseph G. Sheehan (ed.), *Stuttering: Research and Therapy* (New York: Harper & Row, 1970), pp. 172–187.

2. Arthur L. Stinchcombe, "Formal Organizations," in Neil J. Smelser (ed.), *Sociology: An Introduction* (New York: John Wiley, 1967), pp. 150–202.

3. Edwin M. Lemert, *Social Pathology* (New York: McGraw-Hill, 1951), p. 164.

4. Lemert, "Sociological Perspective," *op. cit.*, p. 165.

5. Eliot Freidson, *Profession of Medicine* (New York: Dodd, Mead & Company, 1970), p. 239.

6. Erving Goffman, *Stigma: Notes on the Management of Spoiled Identity* (Englewood Cliffs, N.J.: Prentice-Hall, 1963).

7. J. F. Lofland and R. A. Lejeune, "Initial Interaction of Newcomers in Alcoholics Anonymous: A Field Experiment in Class Symbols and Socialization," in W. F. Filstead (ed.), *Qualitative Methodology* (Chicago: Markham, 1970), pp. 107–118.

8. Herbert H. Hyman and Charles R. Wright, "Trends in Voluntary Association Memberships of American Adults: Replication Based on Secondary Analysis of National Sample Surveys," *American Sociological Review*, vol. 36, no. 2 (April 1971), pp. 191–206. See also M. Hausknecht, *The Joiners* (New York: Bedminster Press, 1962).

10 | Organizational Affiliation and Powerlessness: A Case Study of the Welfare Poor
1. Bernard Berelson and Gary Steiner, *Human Behavior: An Inventory of Scientific Findings* (New York: Harcourt, Brace, 1964), p. 403.
2. Orville G. Brim, Jr., David C. Glass, David E. Lavin, and Norman Goodman, *Personality and Decision Processes: Studies in the Social Psychology of Thinking* (Stanford, Calif.: Stanford University Press, 1962).

11 | Intra-Group Dynamics in Self-Help Organizations
1. Edward Sagarin, *Odd Man In: Societies of Deviants in America* (New York: Quadrangle Press 1969), p. 56.
2. These ideas have been suggested by the writings of Marie Jahoda and Harris Peck. For the former see *Current Concepts of Mental Health* (New York: Basic Books, 1959). For the latter see: "Some Relationships between Group Processes and Mental Health Phenomena in Theory and Practice," *International Journal of Group Psychotherapy*, vol. 13 (1963) and "The Small Group: Core of the Community Mental Health Center," *Community Mental Health Journal*, vol. 4, no. 3 (1968).
3. William B. Cameron, *Informal Sociology: A Casual Introduction to Sociological Thinking* (New York: Random House, 1963), pp. 69–78.
4. Hans Toch, *The Social Psychology of Social Movements* (Indianapolis and New York: Bobbs-Merrill, 1965), p. 73.
5. Sagarin, *op. cit.*, p. 41.

12 | Group Structures and Formats in Self-Help Organizations
1. Bernard Berelson and Gary Steiner, *Human Behavior: An Inventory of Scientific Findings* (New York: Harcourt, Brace & World, 1964), p. 325.
2. Clovis Shepard, *Small Groups: Some Sociological Perspectives* (San Francisco: Chandler Publishing, 1964).
3. Matthew Dumont, "Drug Problems and Their Treatment: Organization of Programs at the State and Local Levels," vol. III, rev. ed., *The American Handbook of Psychiatry* (New York: Basic Books, 1973).
4. Helen Jennings, "The Sociometric Differentiation of the Psychegroup and the Sociogroup," *Sociometry*, vol. 10 (1947).
5. Katherine Whiteside Taylor, *Parents and Children Learn Together* (New York: Columbia University, Teachers College Press, 1967), p. 250.
6. W. R. Bion, "Experiences in Groups," *Human Relations*, vol. I (1948), pp. 314–320, 487–496.
7. Edward Sagarin, *Odd Man In: Societies of Deviants in America* (New York: Quadrangle Press, 1969), chap. 8.
8. Alfred Katz, *Parents of the Handicapped* (Springfield, Ill.: Charles C Thomas, 1961).

13 | Spontaneous or Natural Support Systems
1. Joan Hatch Shapiro, *Communities of the Alone* (New York: Association Press, 1971).
2. Robert Liberman, "Personal Influence in the Use of Mental Health Resources," *Human Organization*, vol. 24 (1965), pp. 231–235.

3. Gerald Caplan, "Patterns of Parental Response to the Crisis of Premature Birth: A Preliminary Approach to Modifying Mental Health Outcome," *Psychiatry,* vol. 23 (1960), pp. 365–374.

4. Phyllis Rolfe Silverman, "The Widow-to-Widow Program. An Experiment in Preventive Intervention," *Mental Hygiene,* vol. 53, no. 3 (1969), pp. 333–337.

5. *Webster's New World Dictionary of the American Language* (Cleveland and New York: World, 1964).

6. Joint Circular from Department of Education and Science, Ministry of Health, Home Office, Ministry of Housing and Local Government, London, England, April 26, 1968.

7. Matthew P. Dumont, "Drug Problems and Their Treatment," in Gerald Caplan (ed.), Section on Adolescent Psychiatry of Volume II, rev. ed., *American Handbook of Psychiatry* (New York: Basic Books, 1973).

8. Robert S. Weiss, "Materials for a Theory of Social Relationships," in *Interpersonal Dynamics,* (eds.) Bennis, Schein, Steele and Berlew (Homewood, Ill.: Dorsey Press, 1968).

15 | Power and Collective Self-Help

1. Sydney Lens, *Poverty: America's Enduring Paradox* (New York: Thomas Y. Crowell, 1971).

2. Conference on Economic Progress, *Poverty and Deprivation in the United States* (Washington, D.C., 1962).

3. Leonard Freedman, *Public Housing* (New York: Holt, Rinehart and Winston, 1969).

4. Department of Commerce, *Current Population Reports, Consumer Series,* No. 78 (1969), p. 60.

16 | Consciousness-Raising: Self-Help in the Women's Movement

1. Robin Morgan (ed.), *Sisterhood Is Powerful* (New York: Random House, 1970).

2. Pamela Allen, *Free Space, A Perspective on the Small-Group in Women's Liberation* (New York: Times Change Press, 1970), p. 4.

3. *Ibid.,* p. 17.

4. *Ibid.,* p. 22.

5. *Ibid.,* p. 36.

18 | Camphill Villages

1. Carlos Pietzner (ed.), "Aspects of Curative Education" (Aberdeen, Scotland: Aberdeen University Press, 1966).

2. *The Cresset,* vol. XV, no. 3 (1969).

3. Rudolf Steiner, "Anthroposophy and the Social Question" (New York: Anthroposophic Press).

Note: The above works are available through The St. George Book Service, P. O. Box 225, Spring Valley, N.Y. 10977.

21 | Self-Help and Mutual Aid in the People's Republic of China
1. Theodore Shabad, *China's Changing Map* (New York: Praeger, 1972), p. 78.
2. Tillman Durdin, "China Stressing Food Production," *The New York Times,* June 24, 1973.
3. Richard H. Solomon, *Mao's Revolution and the Chinese Political Culture* (Berkeley: University of California Press, 1971), p. 37.
4. Mark Selden, *The Yenan Way in Revolutionary China* (Cambridge, Mass: Harvard University Press, 1971), p. 243.
5. Franz Schurmann, *Ideology and Organization in Communist China* (Berkeley: University of California Press, 1970), p. 415.
6. *Ibid.*, p. 404.
7. Selden, *op. cit.*, pp. 246–248.
8. Schurmann, *op. cit.*, p. 420.
9. *Ibid.*, p. 421.
10. Selden, *op. cit.*, p. 246.
11. C. K. Yang, "The Chinese Family in the Communist Revolution," in *Chinese Communist Society: The Family and the Village* (Cambridge, Mass.: MIT Press, 1965), p. 5.
12. Schurmann, *op. cit.*, p. 427.
13. Mao Tse-tung, *Selected Works, Vol. I* (Peking: Foreign Languages Press, 1967), p. 170.
14. *Ibid.*, pp. 299–300.

22 | Self-Help Groups and the Organized Society: A Stocktaking and Excursus
1. Kurt W. Back, *Beyond Words, the Story of Sensitivity Training and the Encounter Movement* (New York: Russell Sage Foundation, 1972), pp. 234–235.
2. Matthew Dumont, "Drug Problems and Their Treatment: Organization of Programs at the State and Local Levels," vol. III, rev. ed., *The American Handbook of Psychiatry* (New York: Basic Books, 1973).
3. Harold L. Wilensky and Charles N. Lebeaux, *Industrial Society and Social Welfare* (New York: Russell Sage Foundation, 1958), p. 141.

Index